THE

CURE

FOR

HATE

THE

CURE

FOR

HATE

A FORMER WHITE SUPREMACIST'S

JOURNEY FROM

VIOLENT EXTREMISM

TO RADICAL COMPASSION

TONY McALEER

ARSENAL PULP PRESS
VANCOUVER

ARSENAL PULP PRESS
Suite 202—211 East Georgia St.
Vancouver, BC V6A 1Z6
Canada
arsenalpulp.com

The publisher gratefully acknowledges the support of the Canada Council for the Arts
and the British Columbia Arts Council for its publishing program, and the Government of
Canada, and the Government of British Columbia (through the Book Publishing Tax Credit
Program), for its publishing activities.

Arsenal Pulp Press acknowledges the xʷməθkʷəy̓əm (Musqueam), Sḵwx̱wú7mesh (Squamish), and səl̓ilwətaʔɬ (Tsleil-Waututh) Nations, speakers of Hul'q'umi'num'/Halq'eméylem/
hən̓q̓əmin̓əm̓ and custodians of the traditional, ancestral, and unceded territories where our
office is located. We pay respect to their histories, traditions, and continuous living cultures
and commit to accountability, respectful relations, and friendship.

Cover and text design by Oliver McPartlin
Edited by Shirarose Wilensky
Copy edited by Linda Pruessen
Proofread by Alison Strobel

Printed and bound in Canada

Library and Archives Canada Cataloguing in Publication:
Title: The cure for hate : a former white supremacist's journey from violent extremism to
radical compassion / Tony McAleer.
Names: McAleer, Tony, 1967– author.
Identifiers: Canadiana (print) 20190122870 | Canadiana (ebook) 20190122951 | ISBN
9781551527697 (softcover) | ISBN 9781551527703 (HTML)
Subjects: LCSH: McAleer, Tony, 1967– | LCSH: Extremists—Canada—Biography. |
LCSH: White Aryan Resistance. | LCSH: White supremacy movements—Canada. | LCSH:
Racism—Canada. Classification: LCC FC104 .M33 2019 | DDC 320.56/9—dc23

This book is dedicated to all the men and women that I have caused harm to in the past that I may not have the opportunity to address. I am truly sorry for the harm I have caused.

In loving memory of Stephen Francis

"Hate is too great a burden to bear.
I have decided to love."
—Martin Luther King Jr., "Where Do We Go from Here?"
address delivered at the eleventh annual Southern Christian
Leadership Conference, August 16, 1967

CONTENTS

FOREWORD

IT'S SAID THAT HISTORY never repeats itself, but it does rhyme. In our
current moment, with the return of xenophobic ideologies and eerily familiar
far-right symbolism, we are forced to wonder what history has in store for
us next. How could so many ordinary people be swayed by discredited and
violent ideas? Even if we are personally averse to discrimination and cruelty,
will our friends and neighbours refrain?

I've been lucky enough to know Tony McAleer for years, and in such
a bewildering time as ours, we need a reliable guide like him. Because our
era prizes excess over expertise, we need to hear from those who know the
mindset of the loudest and most extreme voices, and who can advise us on
how to penetrate the noise and reach the hearts that can be reached. Although
you might not guess it by merely looking at us, Tony and I have more than
one thing in common: we are committed to understanding hate, educating
about hate, and eradicating hate, using the most cutting-edge research and
the power of our own very different stories.

It's remarkable that, despite our vastly separate backgrounds, Tony and I
have arrived at a point of deep agreement—that all extremisms, regardless of
their varying language and symbols, are overwhelmingly similar. Whether
from the far right or far left, whether religious or secular, extremist ideologies
reveal the same core traits, such as an "us versus them" mentality, a rewriting
of history and religious doctrine, and a profound victim complex. In my own
experience, I have witnessed how prejudice against Muslim communities
has been exploited by extremist recruiters, who poison the minds of young
people—usually religious novices—to believe that the defence of their own
people requires violence against others. I have seen the great tradition of Islam
weaponized for political purposes by groups such as Al Qaeda and Daesh,

and by their far-right counterparts who share an equally impoverished view of the faith of 2 billion people. Like Tony, I see the need to explain these fanatical trends without excusing them.

This book offers a close-up example of how prejudice, propaganda, and, especially, shame create an environment in which such a weaponization of ideas can thrive. It is no accident that white supremacist extremists portray themselves as proud, militant, and unstoppable—as Tony explains, this is precisely the technique that allows so many of them to cover up their history of childhood trauma and societal powerlessness that they have internalized for years. In the same way, I have seen extremist fringes of the wide Muslim world attempt to compensate for the collective dishonour of colonization, demonization, and discrimination. When people are treated as if they do not deserve love, they are at risk of seeking false love in the camaraderie of gang violence and cultish isolation. By recounting the details of this process in his own life, Tony enlivens an academic subject with his vital testimony.

Most importantly, Tony offers us lessons for how to turn the tide of radicalization, one person at a time. Through his own disengagement from violent politics, and through the exceptional work of Life After Hate, he shows us that the best methods of counter-extremism involve the very principles of human dignity, radical compassion, and honest justice that the lost seek to undermine. With such wisdom in our tool kit, we do not need to be dominated by fear and fanaticism, and together we can write the next chapter of history.

Daisy Khan
July 2019
Executive editor, WISE Up: Knowledge Ends Extremism
Author, Born with Wings: The Spiritual Journey of a Modern Muslim Woman
Founder, Women's Islamic Initiative in Spirituality and Equality

INTRODUCTION

HIS FORCED SMILE AND desire to crack jokes didn't hide his discomfort, so I got to the point.

"Look, Tony," I said, "we only have an hour, and you've spent the first fifteen minutes doing your best not to say something, something I think you really want to say. So let's stop wasting both of our time. I'm here to help, assist, even guide, but I can't do that if you don't tell me why you're here."

Tony fake-smiled again, and his gaze moved toward the floor, as if somewhere on the carpet he might find the courage to speak the unspeakable. At that moment, I knew he wasn't just uncomfortable; he was ashamed.

We sat silently for almost a full minute, and then his eyes flashed up to my face, as if to make sure I was still there. I gave him a gentle smile and watched his throat move up and down as if he were trying to swallow a golf ball.

Then he opened his mouth and confessed to me who he had been and what he had done. When he was finished, I broke into a huge grin. His expression changed from shy shame to raging anger.

"What are you laughing at?" he demanded.

Once again, I smiled. "You do know I was born Jewish, right?" I said.

"Oh, fuck, you have got to be kidding me!" His anger turned to a sheepish grin, and thus our journey together began.

Many years later, Tony and I sat onstage in New York City as part of a panel at a joint United Nations and US State Department event. The adjudicator turned to me and asked, "Was it difficult for you as a Jewish person to choose to work with Tony?"

"Not really," I replied.

The adjudicator looked more than a little surprised. "Can you tell us why that wasn't difficult for you?"

I answered honestly. "I am honoured to have worked with billionaires who run large organizations. I've worked with street kids and drug dealers. I've worked with people in political office, Olympians, and entertainers. I've worked with people who've told me I'm the best thing that's ever happened to them, and I've worked with people who have suggested that I go copulate with myself. Here's what I've learned: everyone who has ever sat in front of me is a reflection of me. That includes Tony."

The adjudicator seemed puzzled. "Are you saying that you have been a Neo-Nazi, and that's why you could help Tony?"

I explained, "No, I'm saying that everyone who sits in front of me is in some form a reflection of who I was, who I am, or what I contain within me. I was never a neo-Nazi, but that was the symptom in Tony and not a cause." I continued, "When Tony sat in front of me, it would have been easy to see and judge him on the surface of what he'd been, but from my point of view, that was merely the outward expression of something deeper."

"So what did you see?" the adjudicator asked.

"I saw an extremely intelligent man who was looking for significance. I saw a boy in a man's body who desperately wanted to been seen and validated. I saw someone who desperately wanted to belong and to know that he was loved and accepted. I saw a man who lacked any real compassion for the child he had been. I saw a man I could teach to find that compassion. And, yes, I could see that a reflection of who I had been less than twenty years before sat in my office."

You may be reading this book because you are standing on the edge, about to step away from a lifestyle you've outgrown, but you fear leaving what you know. I understand how difficult it can be to walk away from something, even when we rationally know it's unhealthy or dysfunctional. It's particularly difficult if that's where we believe we've been accepted and loved.

You may be reading this book because you have a loved one who seems lost in hate and anger. Or you may be reading this because you find yourself looking out into the world, and you see the rise in tribalism and the dehumanization of certain groups of individuals, and you are trying to understand why anyone would or could buy into a doctrine of hate.

Let me offer you a little guidance on your journey through these pages. As you read this book, consider opening your heart with the compassion to understand that only *hurt people hurt people.* Try to remember that we all want and need love, attention, and a sense of belonging. If we can't get those things in a positive form, we'll take them in the form available. If you are brave enough, have compassion and ask, *What of myself can I see within these pages?*

One final thought: In a time when it's in vogue to talk about finding one's purpose, remember that true purpose is born of darkness. It is only by being willing to know and face our own darkness that we can learn where we are most qualified to bring light to a hurting world.

Dōv Baron
June 2019
Dōv Baron is a best-selling author, twice cited as one of Inc.com's Top 100 Leadership Speakers. He was also named one of the Top 30 Global Leadership Gurus. He works with high-performing individuals and organizations to create purpose-driven companies led by purpose-driven people who are committed to creating a legacy.
fullmontyleadership.com

CHAPTER 1
CHILDHOOD

BEFORE THE SHAVED HEAD and Doc Martens; before the anger and street violence; before the anti-immigrant rhetoric, the Holocaust denial, the white supremacist phone line; before the pain and loneliness—there was Little Tony. Who was that little boy? That core essence deep down inside? Little Tony was an open, bright, sensitive, curious, shy, stubborn, mischievous, and funny little fellow who was open to the wonder of the world around him.

I grew up in the comfortable Dunbar area of Vancouver, Canada, a quiet middle-class neighbourhood with large yards and wide boulevards lined with cherry blossoms in the spring. I was one of a dozen or so kids on the block, playing hide-and-seek or street hockey or football together until the sun went down. By the time I was an adult, Dunbar was home to some of the most expensive real estate in the country.

My father was a doctor, but not just any doctor; he was a psychiatrist. A shrink, or in English slang, a trick cyclist. Have you ever heard the expression about the cobbler's kids who go without shoes? The way my father showed his love for his family was to be a great provider, and we never went without food, clothes, or shelter. But what do you think the psychiatrist's kids go without? I wish I could blame my choices on something so simple. Sadly, I cannot.

I do not blame my childhood for any of the things I did. I made my choices, and I am not a victim. To claim victimhood implies that I had no agency, but the truth is I had plenty of it. I take responsibility for my actions and hold myself accountable for the horrible and evil things that I said and did.

Have you ever been to the grocery store when you were really hungry? Did you notice that when you are starving, the buying choices you make are a little different than if you arrive with a full stomach? You shop more from the middle aisles, where the junk food is, food with very little nutrition that gives you only a fleeting moment of satisfaction. Nobody forces you to put the chips or the cookies in your cart, and you know deep inside that they're not the healthiest choices. But it seems the hungrier you are, the more compelling the little voice in your head that rationalizes the purchase. Ultimately, however, you have a choice; you have agency. As a young man, I went out into the world emotionally hungry, and I made abysmal decisions that damaged not only myself but, more importantly, many, many other people. I made choices that felt good for a fleeting moment but were utterly empty.

So why did I do it? How did a middle-class doctor's kid end up a violent white supremacist? More importantly, how did he come back from that hateful place and return to humanity? And what can others learn from such a journey? I suppose we must go back to the beginning, to my childhood, to find out.

My roots lie not in Canada but in the northwest of England, in Liverpool and its neighbour St Helens, an industrial town known for glassmaking and rugby. I was born in Chesterfield, Derbyshire. Want to know where Chesterfield is? Take your finger and point to the exact spot you think is the middle of England and you will probably hit the crooked church spire for which the town is so famous. I was born there in 1967 while my father was doing his residency at the local hospital, and I was only there for six months or a year before we were back living in Liverpool with relatives. England in the early 1970s was a pretty bleak place with a stagnant economy. Land of opportunity it was not; hence, my dad, and a generation of doctors like him, set their sights elsewhere. My father escaped to the western edge of the Commonwealth and settled in Lotusland—Vancouver, British Columbia.

My father went first, and my mother and I followed. We ended up at the Wagon Wheel Motel near Riverview psychiatric hospital (back when there were still places called asylums, where patients were treated with electroshock therapy—think *One Flew Over the Cuckoo's Nest*). The first place in Vancouver we called home was a two-bedroom apartment two blocks from Kitsilano Beach. My only toys were Gerry the Giraffe and Teddy. Gerry was a painted wooden giraffe on four hollow red plastic wheels that served as my primary mode of transportation. When I wasn't on Gerry, I was with Teddy, my bright yellow furry stuffed bear with brown velvet ears and luminescent orange eyes. I still have Teddy, though he's lost an eye in his travels.

To keep me entertained, my mother used to take me for long rides and day trips on the bus, as we didn't have a car or a TV. My favourite place was the beach, where there was an old steam train engine. I would climb all over it, pretending to be the conductor, shovelling imaginary coal into the furnace and pulling different levers as I imagined billowing clouds of steam and made my own *choo-choo* sounds with childish excitement. (Coincidentally, this steam engine was built in the north of England, not far from where I was born.) Near the beach was the H.R. MacMillan Space Centre, with a giant metallic crab sculpture that burst with spray from the fountain inside. The shallow pool surrounding the crab was filled with coins tossed in by people making wishes and seemed like a gold mine to me. I was always trying to figure out how I could retrieve the treasure without getting wet. Many a day was spent in the expanse of my gigantic playground by the ocean, and in the winter the beach was deserted, leaving Gerry and me in charge. I used to fantasize that the entire beach was my domain, even going so far as to get annoyed when springtime came and people started to trespass on my territory and other kids climbed on my train.

My other favourite place growing up was Second Beach in Stanley Park. Lured by the smell of french fries, my mom and I would visit the concession and feast on the greasy, salty, vinegary goodness until all that was left was the stain at the bottom of the rectangular grey cardboard container. After that came the bus ride through downtown, where we had to change buses to get back to Kitsilano. Near the transfer point was a large department store, the Hudson's Bay Company, and now it was time for my mom to have a little fun. I didn't realize at the time that watching me at play all day was as dull for her as it was for me to watch her browse for women's clothing. With well-timed visits to the toy department and sugary bribes in the form of Jell-O cubes with whipped cream in the store's cafeteria, my mother would maximize her shopping time. In my boredom, I sought adventure exploring the department store, often beyond the reach of my distracted mother. Once, a store clerk thought I was lost and escorted me to the store's administration offices. A loud voice came over the PA system calling for the mother of Tony to go to the office and collect him. While I was waiting, they gave me candy, which was a big mistake, as they were unwittingly rewarding my behaviour and ensuring the repetition of my escapades. This is the first instance I can think of when I figured out how to game the system. In the end, my mother resorted to placing me in a full torso harness with a leash attached. Some people would think it cruel and unusual indeed to treat a child like a dog or other domesticated animal. Sometimes, though, she forgot the harness and I would escape unshackled.

After a while, the novelty of the free candy wore thin and I set my sights on greater adventure, leaving the safety of the store to venture out into the bustle of downtown, where, on one occasion, I found a new group of friends. My mother, panicking when she was unable to find me at the usual spots, began to search outside on the busy street. I hadn't wandered far from the store's main entrance, and she found me with a tambourine, jiving with members of the Hare Krishna religious sect as they chanted and drummed in their orange robes.

I learned to explore and push the limits and boundaries whenever possible, while always being kept relatively safe and close at the same time. As long as I knew where my mother was, I was okay, I thought. Life was simple, carefree, and full of fun and adventure, and I quite enjoyed being the centre of my universe.

In 1971, we moved from that apartment and my kingdom by the sea into the house in Dunbar, which would be my home until I moved out as an adult.

Where was my dad in all of this? Working. I thought the world of him, perhaps because he worked so hard and long to provide for us. Most weeknights I was in bed before he came home. I would try as hard as I could to stay awake, hoping to hear him return through the front door. Most of the time, I had fallen asleep by the time he got home. Often, he would bring treats, but it was the records he thought I might like that got me the most excited. The scarcity of his presence made the time I had with him that much more valuable.

We would travel to England just about every summer for a

month or so and stay with my mother's parents. The reality of our family vacations was that my father couldn't last for more than a day or two before taking off on his own adventures into Liverpool, and I wouldn't see him again until we were back in Vancouver. My dad's family was considered the dysfunctional Irish drinking side, whereas my mom's side was the delightful tea-and-crumpets crowd. I can see in retrospect why my dad didn't socialize well with them.

One year we went to Wales to stay in a little cabin by the beach. Welsh seaside holidays left quite a bit to be desired regarding weather and climate. Maui it was not. But it was novel to me. There was a small shop that catered to those who were intent on spending time by the sea. The store offered an assortment of sunglasses, beach balls, butterfly nets, windmills, and more. There was a lot to keep the youngsters entertained. I settled on an Action Man figure (England's version of G.I. Joe) that came with a deep-sea diving suit complete with a helmet that had a round hinged opening for the face—complete with glass—and heavy lead boots. Attached at the back were small flexible plastic tubes to blow into so that Action Man would release bubbles underwater, like a real scuba diver.

During the last half of the week there was torrential rain, and the central courtyard where we were staying started to flood when the drains reached capacity. While guests huddled inside wondering if the water was going to rise above the door sill, I was having the time of my life outside where there were plenty of deep pools for a four-year-old and his Action Man to go scuba diving. Eventually, the rain subsided, the pools and puddles disappeared, and everything returned to normal.

After almost a week had passed, my dad came wheeling up in a brand-new MG sports car purchased from the factory in Cowley, near Oxford. A new little roadster would be making the trip back to Canada by boat, and I was most excited. As usual, though, my dad could only handle a night or two on holiday with us before he felt compelled to leave. I remember waving goodbye to him sadly, pretending to be excited so as to not disappoint him with my own disappointment. But no matter how hard I tried, I couldn't swallow that lump in my throat. Wearing his new Panama hat, waving and tooting the horn of his new purchase, he sped off into the English countryside to pick up his best friend for an adventure in the South of France.

With the sunshine back, the families returned to playing in the sand, flying kites, and wandering along the shoreline as the cold waves lapped at our feet. I was still hurt and yearning for my father. I walked up to a pair of smiling and laughing siblings who had each built their own sandcastle. I deliberately marched through and obliterated both of the laboriously constructed creations. Their tears mirrored what I felt inside but was too ashamed to show.

There's an old saying: "There is nothing more English than an Englishman abroad." What that means is that Englishmen separated from their ancestral homeland exaggerate their Englishness to a) feel more connected to England and b) make sure their Englishness hasn't been diluted in their time outside the British Empire. This describes my dad to a T.

After a few years in our new house, he decided to renovate the basement and garage into a living space—more precisely, an English pub. The finished result was the envy of every expat who visited. The copper-topped L-shaped bar sat on top of barrels cut in half vertically with the rounded side facing outward and the inside used for storage. Relics from English pubs adorned·the room, with a magnificent collection of vintage mirrors as the backdrop for posters and advertisements for cigarettes, cigars, whiskey, and ales (many no longer in production). There was a stuffed owl wearing my father's old English schoolboy cap, a ship's clock, and a ship's bell (never rung for last call but occasionally to signal another round). Against the opposite wall was a piano that was played regularly, especially during drunk singalongs, and in the corner the old guitar my dad used to play when he was in a band to help pay his way through medical school in Edinburgh.

In the 1970s, the local beer selection in Vancouver was considered to be vastly inferior to the enormous range of ales back in Old Blighty, so my dad set out to brew his own. I remember walking in the door on some weekends and being hit with the steamy aroma of boiling hops that filled the house—an unpleasant smell for someone my age but one I definitely acquired a taste for as I grew older. Cracking his own barley and importing malt from England along with the hops, my father was determined to end the drought of decent ale. After much trial and error, he probably brewed some of the best beer in the city, which was confirmed by the weekly congregation of his expat medical colleagues at what came to be known as the Sunday session, or "sesh." Since you couldn't buy alcohol on Sundays in those days, my dad's five-gallon barrels, powered by little metallic carbon dioxide cartridges, ensured the draft kept flowing on that sacred day.

Curiosity, awe, and the desire to be among the menfolk as they solved the world's problems led me to develop a general knowledge far beyond my age. Most importantly, I learned the art of repartee. The weekly event was quite the heady mix for a young boy, listening as my father and his friends challenged each other's medical knowledge with a mystery diagnosis, recited poetry and literature from memory, vented about women, and expressed jingoistic political views through the lens of their war-child generation. Seldom did they agree on anything, but that was the point. The session wasn't about gentle, polite conversation but, rather, passionate, humorous, sarcastic, and often verbally violent jousting among men who loved to argue and could give as good as they got. They were all competent gladiators in this arena, but none more so than my dad.

My dad was my idol. I admired everything he did and took as gospel everything he said. My trust in him was absolute, and everything I did was an attempt to please him.

When I was five, I asked my mom what I could do for my dad while he was away at work. We settled on shining all of his shoes. Under the kitchen sink was an old cigar box that held the polish (boy, did I love the smell of shoe polish), cloths, and many brushes (for all the different colours). My mom carefully showed me what to do. I set upon the task slowly and diligently with the cloth, the brush, and a bit of spit, shining every one of his dozen or so pairs of shoes. It's not that my dad had an extensive collection of shoes to keep up with the latest in footwear fashion; he just never threw his old ones away.

About two hours later, beaming with pride, I called, "Mom, I'm finished!" and waited for her inspection, which I passed with flying colours. I couldn't wait for my dad to come home for lunch (he was now in an office much closer to home), and when he did, I sprinted to the door to greet him.

"Daddy, Daddy, come and see what I did for you!" I said in anticipation of acknowledgment and praise.

That is not what happened, however. Instead, tears welled up in his eyes and he began to cry.

Confused and unsure, I asked, "Dad, what's wrong? Why are you crying?"

He replied, "Nobody has ever done something this nice for me."

The spontaneity of my gift had caught him by surprise, and for the first time in my life, I caught a glimpse of the sorrow and deep pain he carried below the surface.

As for my mother, she had been a flight attendant before my birth—back in the day when they were known as "sexy stews." She was recruited from her hometown of St Helens to fly out of New York for Trans World Airlines (TWA). In those days, the airlines hired almost solely on looks, and each had its own particular image. TWA favoured the brunette college girl next door; Pan Am had the blonde Swedish look. Carriers such as Canada's Wardair demanded not only that stewardesses wear heels on duty but also that they fit into their uniform, or they couldn't fly. Usually, the uniform only came in one size! Upon pregnancy, my mom was forced to retire.

When I was seven, however, my mom returned to her career, albeit with the small regional carrier Pacific Western Airlines. When I was ten, she left for her first overnight trip. That night, not feeling well, I went to bed early. At about 1:30 a.m., I woke up with a sore throat and a slight fever. I got out of bed and made my way downstairs to the kitchen to get a soothing drink of Ribena (blackcurrant syrup) mixed with water, my childhood beverage of choice. I opened the fridge, grabbed the bottle, and walked over to the sink, but the sticky dried syrup had sealed the cap closed beyond the strength of my small hands. First with one hand and then the other, I twisted the cap as hard as I could until it felt like my skin was going to tear off. As I stood in frustrated silence, I noticed the sound of music coming from my dad's bar downstairs. *I'm in luck!* I thought. *Dad is still up, probably drinking with one or two of his friends.*

I quietly descended the stairs. To the left was a wooden door with a window that led to the renovated bar. Curiously, I peered through the glass to see which friend my dad was with. The person I saw was not one I recognized, as all of his drinking buddies were male. This friend was female, not my mother, and not wearing any clothes.

As I stood there frozen in disbelief, my ten-year-old brain tried to process what it was witnessing. Immediately, I was overcome with a flood of emotions: shame, anger, guilt, and, most of all, betrayal. I could feel the blood rushing to my cheeks, and the churning in my stomach became a raging tempest of feelings—the ones that are not joyful; the ones that frighten, that itch and scream for relief; the ones that make your mind scramble for the Stop button, unable to find it.

Rocked to my core, I snapped out of it and ran upstairs. I put the Ribena bottle down on the kitchen table, sat in a chair, and sobbed. My whole world had turned upside down. At that moment, the father I so idolized, who could do no wrong in my eyes, fell off his pedestal.

My dad must have heard me because he soon appeared at the top of the stairs.

"How could you do that to my mother!" I shouted, feeling the anger not only of my own betrayal but also of my mom's.

My father asked me if I wanted to meet the woman.

Incredulous, with a snarl, I answered, "No!"

"What are you going to do?" he asked, realizing that his marriage was likely on the line.

"Tell Mom," I responded confidently.

"You know she could divorce me over this?" he asked, a note of nervousness in his voice.

"She has the right to know" was my response.

I handed him the Ribena bottle, which he opened for me, and I went to the sink, made my drink in silence, gulped it back to relieve my throat, and went to bed.

Two days later, I told my mom.

On a continent thousands of miles away from home and any

real support, in an era when divorce laws were not as progressive as they are today, my mother made one of the most difficult decisions of her life and decided to keep the family intact, albeit in separate bedrooms.

CHAPTER 2
SCHOOL DAYS

IN PRESCHOOL AND KINDERGARTEN, I enjoyed myself but was somewhat socially awkward. When the other kids were reading I was painting, and when they were painting I was reading. I did the opposite of everybody else but not in a disruptive way. I often found myself—correction: placed myself—on the outside.

Before my father's betrayal, school was enjoyable, and for the most part, I participated fully. I was invested in doing well, even if in an unorthodox way, and often found myself among the top of the class. But after that night, everything changed. As that year ended and grade six began, my marks began to slide, dropping from solid As and Bs down to Cs and C-minuses.

The school I went to was Vancouver College, an all-boys Catholic school from kindergarten to grade twelve run by an Irish order known as the Christian Brothers. The Christian Brothers were not priests, but they dressed in black and wore a priest's white collar. The school tried to motivate me with all kinds of different incentives, sending me to science fairs and on trips to special events, but to no avail. I was tuning out. Acting out and becoming the class clown became my focus as I sought out negative attention. Anything to be seen.

After several months Brother Gianti requested a meeting with my parents to try to overcome my resistance to turning my grades around. I wasn't just resisting learning—this was the beginning of me resisting everything. The solution that all parties except me agreed to was quite simple; I believe it was even my father's suggestion: "Why not just beat the grades into him?"

To me, it seemed as if Brother Gianti was a little too eager to carry out my father's request.

What did that look like?

One day, the teacher came in after the break with a stack of marked exams. He lectured the class on the need to do better as he placed each student's exam facedown on their desk. The suspense was killing me as he delivered mine. As if I were playing a game of Texas hold 'em, I curled a corner of the test up until my score was revealed: sixty-three percent. Damn. My stomach sank. I knew what that mark meant.

"Tony, go wait for me outside my office," the teacher said.

I rose to my feet and forced my trembling legs forward with a growing sense of dread as I shuffled slowly out of the classroom, turned right, and kept going down the hall to sit and wait on one of the two small chairs outside Brother Gianti's door. Whether I had to wait five minutes or ten before he came, I always wished for one or two minutes more. As the teacher walked the hundred or so feet from the classroom toward me, I felt a sense of impending doom that increased with each footstep he took. When he arrived at his office, he looked down at me and fumbled for the keys in his pocket before pulling them out, inserting the right key in the lock, and pushing the door open. He ushered me in ahead of him before closing the door.

He sat down behind his desk in the small office and started to remind me why I was there (like I didn't know). Standing before him, eyes cast downward, focusing on the metal nameplate that sat just before the edge of the desk, I wanted to be anywhere but in that room. Anywhere but there. His lecture always ended with the same line: "This is going to hurt me more than it's going to hurt you." I'd like to get my hands on the person who first came up with that bold lie. I am not sure who it was meant to comfort, but it wasn't me.

"Hands on the desk and assume the position," he ordered.

I leaned over with my arms outstretched and placed my hands on the edge of the desk to stop myself from falling over. He walked over to the corner and selected his favourite tool (a piece of wood about three feet long, two inches wide, and three-quarters of an inch thick), took his usual stance behind me and to the side, and lined up his first shot.

Whack!

The sound registered before the sensation, and then searing pain shot through me before I could fully and adequately process what was happening to my body. I felt the sting return—

Whack!

I can get through this, I thought, as he lined up another blow. Squirming almost involuntarily in anticipation as he swung his arm back, I thrust my hips forward in a feeble attempt to minimize the pain through physics, to reduce the velocity of that piece of wood hitting my rear. Sometimes it worked, but only to necessitate a "redo."

Whack!

I wanted to be anywhere other than in that room with that man, but I was powerless to change my circumstance. As I accepted the complete hopelessness of my situation, my eyes welled up and I fought back the tears in an attempt to retain what little control I had left over my body.

Whack!

But I couldn't manage to keep control of the crying, and I started bawling my eyes out.

Whack! Whack!

Sobbing and pleading, I begged for it to stop, totally surrendering to his will.

Finally, it ended.

No matter how many times I returned to that office, the punishment never exceeded eight strokes. Unlike some of the other victims of the Christian Brothers, I was lucky enough to keep my pants on. To this day, I don't think I have ever felt more powerless than I did in that office, over and over and over again.

Returning to class, I tried to hide my tears, but my red face gave me away. The tough kids would return from such a session with no tears and a "That's all you got?" smirk on their faces. Not me. My cheeks reddened further as I felt additional shame wash over me at the slight laughs and snickers my display of weakness earned. I was eleven.

My grades didn't go up as a result of the beatings, but they continued nonetheless. I even tried to ingratiate myself to the teacher by signing up for extracurricular activities and projects in the hope that he would be more lenient. Nothing worked.

For the next several years, I continued to act out, to coast, and to turn off. I niggled and annoyed my teachers until they lost their cool and blew a gasket on me, which I found particularly rewarding (it was most potent if it happened in front of the class). My thinking was that if I could hijack a teacher's emotional state, then I had control over them, not the other way around. In my juvenile mind, it was a way to flip the power dynamic. This became a pattern that I would repeat over and over again in my life.

I irritated and provoked my way through grades eight and nine. No matter what the school did to try to shift the motivations and punishments, nothing worked. My usual punishment was a Saturday detention, which became a weekly occurrence, and I spent those mornings at the school doing menial outdoor tasks like raking leaves, gardening, and other groundskeeping duties. Week in, week out, rain or shine, I set the school record for the most Saturday detentions in a row, a distinction I wore with pride. Although I was punctual and put in my two hours every Saturday, it can't be said that I was a good worker. I passed the time with as little production as possible, frustrating those who administered my weekly sentence. Obey the rule but ignore the intention—in fact, defy the intention—was how I undermined my teachers.

On one especially dreary Saturday morning in late February, when the rain was torrential and the temperature was just above freezing, I decided the conditions were unbearable. Another indentured servant had also had enough, and together, we meandered back to the school in search of the solace of the hallways' hot water radiators. We sat down and absorbed all the heat they could deliver, rubbing our hands together, our fingers tingling back to life. Meanwhile, the brother who had been searching the grounds to find his workers and inspect their efforts was soon to be disappointed.

The door to the outside burst open and the furious brother stormed into the hallway, bellowing, "What are you doing inside? You should be working!"

"We were too cold and wet to work," we replied.

"These conditions are inhumane!" I added cheekily.

Raging, the brother told us to pick up our things and leave, which we promptly did. Victory! Once again, my stubbornness proved greater than a teacher's will to continue the perpetual battle between us, and he gave up. This filled me with a massive sense of satisfaction, as I had successfully hijacked his emotional state. I had power over him, and it felt damn good in the moment; I didn't have the insight to see that I was really only defeating myself.

That was the last of my Saturday detentions. Several weeks later, my parents and I were called into a meeting with the principal.

"There isn't any one thing that Tony's done worthy of expulsion," he said, "but his general level of defiance is off the charts. We give up. We've tried the carrot and stick, to no avail. We suggest he finish the year, but that you take him to another school next year."

Where would I go next? I wanted to get away from everything in Vancouver and connect with my English roots, so I expressed my desire to return to the United Kingdom and try boarding school.

That spring, my mother and I took a trip to visit half a dozen schools in England, mostly in the middle of nowhere. The one that took my fancy was Scarborough College, set in a scenic North Yorkshire seaside resort. "Seaside resort" is a bit of a misnomer. Unlike Cancun, Maui, or Daytona Beach on spring break, Scarborough was cold, craggy, and windy, except for a few months in the summer. Only a lunatic would swim in the North Sea. For me, the charm of the place was that it wasn't Catholic, it was co-ed, and it had a promenade that ran along the length of the beach. Across the road from the beach were shops, cafés, and arcades. Video games and pinball were definitely my thing, and these arcades sealed the deal. In my fourteen-year-old wisdom, I chose my boarding school based on the availability and variety of video game arcades and the presence of the opposite sex.

As the summer of 1982 drew to a close, I set off on my next adventure. With a clean slate, I found myself enjoying my first term at Scarborough College. At least once a month, we had what were known as exeat weekends, when our six-day school week was shortened and we got a full weekend to leave Scarborough and visit family, which I did at every opportunity. I spent my exeat weekends with my maternal grandparents in St Helens. My grandfather would pick me up at the train station after my three-hour journey and bring me home, where all kinds of treats awaited. Also waiting for me in St Helens were the many friends that I had made over the years during my annual summer visits. After enjoying a big meal and spending a little time with my grandparents, I was off into the night to hang out with my buddies.

St Helens was an industrial town in the north of England between Liverpool and Manchester. In the 1980s, it was reeling from the effects of deindustrialization and Thatcherite economics, which attempted to tame soaring inflation and high interest rates at the expense of wage increases, unions, and employment. In a similar situation to the United States, the UK's coal and steel industries were especially stricken. St Helens was also where I was first exposed to the skinhead subculture—the music, the fashion, and the philosophy. Every Friday and Saturday night I was there, all the young people from around Moss Bank (where my grandparents lived) and Clinkham Wood, which separated Moss Bank from the much rougher government housing estates on the other side, would gather at a pedestrian underpass beneath the East Lancashire highway to smoke, drink, listen to music, and banter. The crowd was right out of the movie *This Is England*, an eclectic mix of youth subcultures with a half-dozen skinheads at the core, including a couple of much older guys who never grew up and relished their role as king of the kids. I was drawn to the anger of punk music. Anger was always just below the surface in me, and this was reflected in my listening preferences, which had shifted from Queen and Elton John, two of my dad's favourites, to the Clash and the Sex Pistols, and then started to move to bands that were angrier, harder, faster, and rawer. As for fashion, St Helens was where I bought my very first pair of Doc Marten boots. In my desire to fit in, I started to dress the part, wearing a thick studded belt and a waist-length World War II army coat adorned with studs and all the cool band buttons I could find. A Union Jack was painted on the back. I found myself drawn to the skinhead pride in being working class and pride in their nation. Although some skinheads in London were already flirting with the National Front (NF)—then Britain's leading far-right white nationalist political party—politics hadn't shown up in the music yet, and most skinheads were not racist.

The skinhead youth culture was born in the late sixties in working-class East London, where alienated youth lived alongside Jamaican immigrants listening to reggae and ska. In a rejection of middle-class "hippie" ideals, the East End youth embraced the symbols of working-class culture, and workboots (Doc Martens) and cropped hair became the stylistic hallmarks of skinhead identity. Skinheads were a vibrant, inclusive youth culture long before they became known for racism. Only twenty-five years had elapsed since the end of World War II, and the fervent nationalism that was required to mobilize a war effort and that symbolized the resilience of the East End of London, which bore the brunt of the German bombings during the Blitz, didn't die easily.

I suppose this, too, is where my father's national pride in England originates: the bombing of Liverpool. My father had grown up in the Catholic slums of the city, where Irish immigrants were forced to live in overcrowded housing in a small area near the docks. Having worked at the Tate & Lyle sugar refinery in his youth, he prided himself on his working-class origins. "Middle-class income, working-class roots," he would often boast. I grew up comfortably middle class, but connecting with the working class was a way of connecting with my father by proxy.

When I arrived at Scarborough College, at the age of fifteen, I was placed in the fourth form, the equivalent of grade nine instead of ten, as the British system of education was a year ahead of North America's and I needed to catch up. I adjusted to my new surroundings and participated fully, with vigour and enthusiasm, making new friends and (mostly) fitting in.

I had learned from my father's Sunday sessions with his cronies how to give and get "stick" (slang for the sarcastic banter that the English love insulting each other with). England's great promise to all of its citizens is someone else to look down on, and it works. I'm convinced that's part of how the class system stays intact. Putting each other down with humour, public humiliation, and laughing at friends and foes alike—these skills were absolutely necessary for me to establish myself within the school pecking order.

I lived in a dormitory off the school grounds called Hartford House. Just like in the Harry Potter books, the school had several houses that were in competition with each other throughout the school year in various games and contests. My three roommates were in the fifth form, a grade higher, but they were the same age as me. We got along most of the time, except when Ireland came up. What hadn't occurred to me when I selected my school was that there would be a problem being one of only two Catholics, with an Irish last name, attending a Methodist boarding school. The school was filled with British Army kids whose parents were serving overseas, some in Northern Ireland. What could possibly go wrong?

The Irish question was always a complex one in my family. My mother was English Protestant, and my dad was Liverpool Irish Catholic, so I used to joke that the first thing I did when I woke up in the morning was beat myself up. However, my dad always bought British cars, beer, and tea, and when the World Cup came around, he supported England. The code was confusing but was something akin to Ireland first, except when they couldn't compete. There was a sense of dual loyalty, which was always trumped by the Irish identity. My father frequently reminded me of the discrimination he faced for being Irish and Catholic, and how my great-aunt had been beaten in her Liverpool home with a fireplace poker by members of the Orange Order (an English Protestant fraternal organization) for being Catholic and died of brain damage a few days later. I was raised on the Wolfe Tones and Irish rebel songs.

In England, nobody is called by their real name, and I had two nicknames. The playful but irritating one was "Damn Yank," which played on the trendy jeans of the same name and my Canadian accent, which to my schoolmates sounded American. The more insulted and annoyed I became, the more it was used, and to my chagrin, it stuck. The other was simply "Irish." In the close quarters of the dorm room, my three roommates called me "Irish," and not in an endearing way. My unapologetic support for the republican cause and the Irish Repulican Army (IRA), and my belief that all of Ireland should be an independent republic, led to the deterioration of our relationships. At the end of the term, I got into a heated argument with my biggest roommate, nicknamed "Pooh," after Winnie-the-Pooh, about the Hyde Park bombing by the IRA that had killed some British soldiers and horses on parade. The IRA was in the midst of a terrorist bombing campaign to liberate Northern Ireland from British rule. The British had dispatched the army to the streets of Belfast and beyond to pacify the rebellion.

Pooh had a mostly gentle demeanour, but this day he was in my face, questioning my thoughts, and I was being extremely provocative in response.

"Were they in uniform?" I demanded about the soldiers.

To which Pooh replied, "Yeah, so what? They were on parade!"

Coldly, I responded, "If they were wearing uniforms, then they were legitimate targets."

The next minute was filled with silence as I watched his face turn red with anger. I could see that it took all of his personal control not to knock me out right then and there. I was absolutely shitting my pants, as there was no way I could even begin to hold my own against his size and strength. Luckily for me, he restrained himself.

That was the end of what had become a very tenuous relationship with my roommates, and in the last three weeks or so of the term it was characterized more by silence and dirty looks than anything else. I could feel their disdain for me, but I didn't care (like my conflict with authority figures, this lack of caring was another theme that was beginning to repeat itself), and the tension remained until the Christmas break, which couldn't come soon enough.

After a three-week holiday in Vancouver, I returned to Hartford House and, weary from the day's travel, laboured up the stairs to my room. As I entered, a few things became apparent. My bed was covered in sheets and blankets that weren't mine, my desk was littered with someone else's items, and the chest of my belongings was gone. Pooh was standing there with his arms crossed, staring at me with derision, amused at my perplexed state.

"You need to speak to Mr Wilson," Pooh said.

It seemed quite clear that this was no longer my room. Confused, annoyed, angry, and a little relieved, I wandered down the stairs to Mr Wilson's open door. I knocked, leaned my head in, and saw him at his desk, writing away. He stopped, looked up, and made eye contact. I asked, "You wanted to see me, Mr Wilson?"

"Ah, yes, Tony," he replied, laying his pen down on the desk. He waved me in to sit down across from him and gestured for me to close the door. "We've had some complaints from the other boys in your room, and they have asked me to place you somewhere else. The problem is, the only room with space doesn't want you either."

Understandable, I suppose. What British Army kids would want an Irish Catholic in their midst, never mind one with republican sympathies.

"Where do I go then?" I asked.

"Top dorm," he replied.

With those words, my heart sank deep into the pit of my stomach. I had no response. Gutted and utterly humiliated, I was overcome with the old familiar feelings of shame and rejection. Once again, I was facing punishment that my adolescent brain felt I didn't deserve. Staring at the floor, heartbroken, I received my instructions to collect my things and take my place in the top dorm. To the jeers and snickers of my old roommates, I entered their room, gathered my belongings, and headed back out the door. As I left, I heard them mumbling something I could barely make out. The only word I could detect was "Fenian," a derogatory term for Irish nationalists or Catholics. If they wanted a Fenian revolt, they were about to get one.

Upon entering top dorm, I threw my things down on an open bed and surveyed the room. Top dorm housed twenty-five boys of various ages, from eleven to fourteen. I was disheartened to have to bunk with a bunch of kids who were younger than me; it took the wind right out of my sails and brought me to a complete standstill. But my shame and humiliation were quickly replaced by familiar feelings of anger and defiance. Within a few weeks, I'd formed a union with the top dorm boys, and we began what was to be known as the top dorm rebellion.

Scarborough College, like most English boarding schools, was organized into a strict hierarchy and power structure, starting with the headmaster. Each house had a housemaster too. The bottom four grades were the junior boys (and girls), and the top three were the senior boys (and girls). Sometimes, the senior boys would pick on, tease, or even physically bully the younger boys, doling out dead arms and the like. The worst was having your bedsheet pulled down tight over you so that you couldn't move and resist the blows. Among the most senior boys were the prefects, handpicked and deputized to enforce discipline and order, and dole out punishments, as an extension of the administration. After four years of getting bullied and bossed by the prefects, a boy might have the chance to assume the role of taskmaster himself. This ancient British power structure had been designed to teach obedience in following orders, knowing your station, and accepting your position within a system that churned out students most prepared to serve the British Empire.

However, this conformity to the existing power structure was foreign to me—I suppose that was the Celtic part of me. Quickly, I became known as the ringleader, with a couple of lieutenants, of a gang of twenty-plus kids from top dorm that began undermining authority wherever we could. We put an end to the most egregious bullying by sheer numbers (certainly not by size), and I started to enjoy the power I wielded through others. As ringleader, I also received most of the punishment meted out for our defiance and disobedience. As I had back at Vancouver College, with my Saturday detentions, I started to rack up an impressive number of consecutive punishments—for early bedtimes now—and went on to set the house record. Lights out was at 9:30, but most nights I was in bed at eight. In this state of constant rebellion, I was oft reminded of my Irish paternal grandfather (who had died the year I was at boarding school). As a member of the merchant navy, he had been torpedoed during both world wars, and his favourite expression was "I call no man sir and no place home." I openly adopted the line, as I felt it easily justified my continued pattern of defiance with simple genetics. I had the "angry Celt" disposition down. This was a cocktail of mythology distilled from the ancient history of the Celts. The Romans, armed with a strict hierarchy, military formations, and discipline, fought and conquered everyone they came across—except for the Celts. One of the Celts' strengths was the ferocious way they charged into battle. However, their weakness was the way they all charged into battle as equals, with no leader having authority over another, except the chieftain (and occasional chieftess). "My knee bends to no man" was another of my grandfather's sayings.

So after a bright and promising first term at Scarborough College, the second term was filled with frustration, struggle, and rebellion as I worked through my demotion to top dorm. I couldn't wait to get out of that place at the end of the school year. After the Easter break, I handed Mr Wilson a letter from my parents giving the school notice that I was leaving, which, surprisingly, took him aback. Mr Wilson chuckled when he told my parents about the formation of a union in top dorm under my leadership and admitted he had made a mistake sending me there, as he actually had a fondness for me. There were many attempts to convince me to stay, even the offer of a private room the following year, but they were to no avail. It was time to move on.

CHAPTER 3
ULTRAVIOLENCE

I WAITED NERVOUSLY AS the ticket line inched forward, the crowd slowly shuffling to the entrance. I anxiously looked up and down the line. Kiva, the stylish punk girl I'd met at a party when I was home from Scarborough College for Christmas break, and who had told me about the show, was nowhere to be seen. Out of the corner of my eye, I saw two big skinheads walking from the entrance down the line in my direction. The "small" guy was about five eleven and 160 pounds, and I put the big one at five eight and 220. Both were sporting freshly shaved heads, so close only a razor could have done the job, and matching blue bomber jackets. As for me, I was a lightweight at five nine and 135 pounds sopping wet.

They got closer. The small one elbowed the big one and nodded in my direction. The larger skinhead had Doc Martens, but the smaller one was wearing combat boots. They stopped right in front of me. As the blood drained from my face, my heart started to pound and my limbs trembled. I had encountered people like this before in England. Skinheads both enthralled and scared the shit out of me, with their very predictable unpredictability and their fearsome thirst for violence.

"What size are your feet?" the big guy asked, eyeing my Doc Martens hard.

"Seven and a half," I answered.

It was an outright lie, but I knew why he was asking, and I was literally shaking in my boots. If my shoe size matched either of theirs, I was going to get robbed and have to go home in my socks, like a character in some dark and twisted Cinderella story. (Docs were harder to come by in Vancouver than in England in those days.)

After a tense moment, the big one elbowed the small one. "They wouldn't fit you anyways," he said, shaking his head and motioning for his friend to follow.

As they rounded the corner of the building and headed into the alleyway, I let out a huge sigh of relief, realizing I had just escaped what probably would have been the beating of a lifetime. Little did I know that those two skinheads would soon become my best friends. You see, my bullying survival strategy was to befriend the bully and become the bully. There was safety, I believed, in the eye of the hurricane.

My heart was finally slowing as I stood outside the New York Theatre on Commercial Drive, an iconic rundown building now beautifully restored and no longer host to all-ages punk shows. The excitement, curiosity, and impatience I had been feeling before the Doc Marten incident returned. Black Flag with Henry Rollins was to be my initiation into the Vancouver punk scene. I had been to concerts before, big names like Van Halen and the Kinks, but there was no rebellion in that music. Their lyrics did not call out to my soul with the chorus of a hundred voices just like mine. Their sound wasn't dripping with venom and contempt for the system, that righteous anger resonating with the rage that burned like an ember at the very core of my being. I may not have been consciously aware of the internal source of all that anger (the betrayal, the humiliation, and the beatings), but I could feel it when it was awakened and stoked by the raw driving guitars that supported the disgruntled voices of this lost generation of youth. The music was powerful, the message accessible, and the chorus hard to resist. Wild in the streets, I felt like I belonged to a group, to a rebellion, to a resistance, to a movement when I sang along to the lyrics.

Finally, I reached the front of the line. Inside the theatre, I stood nervously in the shadows and took in the crowd. It was like a scene from *Rudolph the Red-Nosed Reindeer*'s Island of Misfit Toys—these people were the different, rejected, and discarded. I looked around at all the unique expressions of nonconformity in clothing, hairstyles, and makeup. The perfectly spiked hair, foot-long green mohawks, shaved heads; the tartan skirts and torn fishnets; the buttons, badges, and safety pins—just a bunch of kids escaping the mainstream society that didn't accept them. We were the misfits. On the eve of attending my third high school in four years, I had finally found a place where I felt welcome, accepted, and at home.

By the time Henry Rollins took the stage, the atmosphere was electric, and the packed crowd moved and swayed, undulating as one, with the hot dank smell of booze and sweat dripping from the walls. Rollins's performance was intense, his bulging veins growing more prominent as he poured angst from the stage. The music was the soundtrack to our rebellion, and it gave us fuel. This was about us. On that summer night on Commercial Drive, the New York Theatre became the one place where no matter who you were you belonged.

With my ears ringing, I slipped out into the night. My clothing, damp from dancing and sweating in the mosh pit, quickly started to cool, providing relief to my overheated body. I left early to escape the attention of the two skinheads. I had dodged a bullet earlier, but I still wasn't safe as I got on the bus. At home, with my eyes closed and my headphones on, it was like there was a riot right inside my bedroom and all my friends were there.

Over the following weeks, Kiva introduced me to a new circle of friends. It wasn't long before I met the skinheads from the Black Flag show who had almost rolled me for my Docs. We bonded quickly because of my slight English accent (enhanced by my desire to fit in at boarding school and because I was teased for my "American accent") and knowledge of skinheads from my time England, and the three of us became the best of friends.

Elmo (the small one) and FiFi (the big guy) were feared and respected everywhere they went. I tagged along to parties and saw lots of local bands, like D.O.A., Death Sentence, and House of Commons (HOC), to name but a few. I loved the live shows because of the energy and angst. The ever-increasing volume as the crowd grew restless with anticipation while waiting for the band to step onstage, the moment when all the pressure and pent-up energy was released. Then the crowd let out a raucous roar! Feedback from the amps pierced the silence as the band started at full tilt, dropping right into the driving hard-core punk guitars that urged on the raw, gritty, screaming vocals. That was the moment everyone lost control. Every other week I would go to a show to get my fix of this excitement and contagious energy, something I had never experienced before and that compelled me to dive in headfirst.

With hindsight, those early few years look so innocent compared to what would follow. There was a time when punks and skinheads could swim in the same pond, go to the same shows and parties, but there was always tension. We skinheads would build a crew and feed our adrenaline-fuelled need for violence by responding in an over-the-top way to the slightest provocation or sign of disrespect; in our world, respect was everything, and the slightest dis was enough to kick things off. The desire to be provocative was at the centre of it all.

My high school for the final two years until graduation was a public school. The teachers at Prince of Wales didn't seem to care what you did as long as you didn't disrupt the class. There were, however, a few I managed to provoke. Madame Schenkel, the French teacher, had her students choose a French name from a list to be used in class. My choice was Adolphe, from near the top of the list, and I deliberately dropped the *e* when doing work on the chalkboard. At this point, my provocations were driven by the desire to offend, as skinheads had adopted the symbols of the far right without serious attention to the ideology. The symbols were a fashion statement, a way of showing our disdain and utter contempt for mainstream society. Mr Carlson, the social studies teacher, had me sitting at the back of the class surrounded by a buffer of empty desks so that I couldn't disturb my neighbours with my wisecracks. Despite this, the general attitude at the school was a little more laissez-faire than I was used to. As parents weren't cutting cheques to the school, there wasn't as much effort from the teachers or the administration to ensure results. And without teachers invested in forcing me to succeed, there wasn't much for me to rebel against. Confronted with this new reality, I took my rebellion out into the streets and embraced Vancouver's burgeoning skinhead scene.

I was searching for identity and a place to fit in, and when I first returned to Vancouver from England, that identity was much more punk than skinhead. Although I was hanging out with Elmo and FiFi, my boarding school tweed blazer—adorned with nickel-sized pins and badges from all my favourite punk bands—was my jacket of choice (before I bought my first bomber jacket). I was drawn to the skinhead lifestyle, but left-wing and anarchist politics were my initial interest, as reflected in my preference for bands like Crass and D.O.A. Without a school to push back against, the wider world drew my focus; in my provocative way, I even did a school project on the Squamish Five, a left-wing anarchist group that bombed the Dunsmuir power station in British Columbia, causing $5 million in damages, and set of a bomb at Litton Industries in Toronto, which manufactured parts for cruise missile guidance systems.

At this time, there were no cows too sacred to gore. In my irreverence, I rebelled against everything and everyone. If something had value to the majority of people, it was a target for my ridicule and contempt. The punk side of me revelled in rejecting the system and anything associated with it through my childish antics. Everything was swirling around in a giant pool of confusion and hypocrisy, and a search for identity.

As this tug-of-war between identities played out, the intense English working-class skinhead culture started to feel more real and to resonate with me the most. Although my new identity as a punk was thrilling, it wasn't enough. In the days and weeks between shows, I was listening to more and more of the skinhead music that Elmo passed my way. "Oi! Oi! Oi!" by the Cockney Rejects was as song that grabbed me, as did "Chaos" and "Sorry" by the 4-Skins. Something, you see, had shifted: I was no longer searching for an identity but a way of life. The punk identity was open to so much interpretation and creativity, but the skinhead lifestyle had rules, structure, and expectations. I knew exactly what I had to do to belong, to fit in, and to gain that brotherhood and acceptance I craved. At sixteen, I had no clue who I was, but I did know that I wanted some of the same fear and respect that Elmo and FiFi got. With them, I felt safe—safe in the eye of the hurricane. I was no longer torn between identities. I knew who I was becoming—or so I thought.

At that time, I was too busy putting on masks—the emotional armour of disconnection, and the projection of illusions—to know much of anything. The mask I wore for the longest time was, as I now call it, "Dark Tony." This was the mean, angry, nasty, insensitive version of myself. Dark Tony represented all the hate and anger in me, and stood in contrast to Little Tony, who was the light, my essence—the sensitive, shy, bright, and soft little boy who had been hurt in my childhood. Mean and vicious, the bully ego protected the bullied.

When we are children, we are authentic and open until it is no longer safe for us to be that way. As we grow older, we compartmentalize our lives, putting up shields and wearing many masks to disguise who we are. This is especially true when we don't like who we are. We wear some masks to hide, and we wear others to project to the world someone we aren't. I wore many masks, and I invested incredible amounts of energy and time in living what they represented. At the beginning, feeling rejection and its accompanying pain stung like hell, so I became accustomed to using all of my self-control to conceal my hurt and project the image of a person with no feelings. Those feelings were blocked and diverted to an isolated compartment before they had a chance to overwhelm me. After a while, the diversion becomes more automatic and less conscious, until we no longer feel the pain. We become just numb enough so that we are never overwhelmed by it. The more we avoid, the more numb we become.

To dull the pain that snuck through my defences, I self-medicated. Booze became my medicine of choice, and by the age of sixteen or seventeen, I was a teenage drunk. Hurling myself into drunkenness every weekend for an entire year was my goal—and I had no problem achieving it. I would often drink myself legless, waking up bruised from whatever scrap I'd gotten into, with no recollection of the previous evening's events. It would all start innocently enough—with me drinking and having fun like everybody else—but after four or five drinks, the baton would be handed off to Dark Tony. Then came the race to drink to oblivion, and it was there where my rage found no restraint, where I could commit acts of violence I would never consider while sober. Violence was the source of our power, fear, and respect, and that reputation required regular maintenance and activity. Oi! music and modern skinhead culture was all about drinking and fighting, and I found myself gravitating toward a youth subculture that gave me permission to act out my rage.

Another mask I wore helped me to project violence and inspire fear. The more violence I was involved with at parties and at punk shows, the easier it became, the more normal it felt. The intimidating skinhead dress code, complemented by our aggressive and hostile behaviour, transmitted a visible message: "Don't mess with us, as we won't hesitate to get violent." Understandably, people were fearful and intimidated (not everyone; mainly those who didn't speak the language of violence in their daily discourse). Although many of my crew were every bit as ferocious and frightening as their image and reputation suggested, my strength was my brain, not my brawn. Much like the pufferfish or the porcupine, I projected a threat much greater than the reality.

The human mind is capable of incredible intellectual gymnastics when it comes to rationalizing behaviour. I've always needed there to be a justification before lashing out, whether that was a comment, a look, a threat, or even a perceived threat, no matter how tiny. I wouldn't tolerate cruelty to animals, but people? Everybody was guilty of something.

The music I listened to also gave me permission, justification, and the frame of mind to not only commit violence but to also embrace it as a lifestyle. Some of my mates had been introduced to that violence long before Oi! music was ever on the scene, when they were younger and often on the receiving end. Oi! music not only resonated with raw aggression and anger but also amplified it. Being a middle-class west-side kid, I was soft, despite what Dark Tony advertised. For me, the violence was a learned behaviour, whereas my skinhead buddies came by their toughness naturally. I hadn't grown up in a rough neighbourhood, having to dodge blows from parents or siblings, where hitting back was second nature. Quite the opposite. I'd had a sheltered upbringing and was entering the world of violence by choice. If I was to have their protection, I needed to have their respect. And to earn their respect, I would have to join in all of the violence that they committed, which I did most willingly (I was late to the party and had a lot of catching up to do). Through this exchange, I received acceptance when I had felt unlovable, attention when I had felt invisible, and power when I had felt totally weak. I'm not minimizing my role in any of the violence that I initiated or was involved with. This was what I got out of the violence, how it served me, how I used it despite not having the greatest fighting ability. Competent, yes, but a skilled streetfighter? Compared to many of my comrades, the answer is no.

I remember my first fight.

Elmo and I arrived at a party not far from my parents' house. The event was in full swing, but it was invite-only and they weren't letting anybody in, especially not us, in our skinhead uniform of Doc Martens, bomber jackets, and shaved heads. Some guy and his buddy at the door, drunker than we were, started to get mouthy and belligerent.

I can't remember who made the first move, but there was some pushing and shoving, and Elmo and I squared off with the two door guys. One of them swung at me and missed my nose by an inch, so I swung back, but I missed too! He missed because he was drunker than me, but I missed because I was clumsy and inexperienced.

The adrenaline was pumping. I felt anxious, with fear and excitement welling up from within. My hands took two fistfuls of his hair, pulling his face down to meet my rapidly rising knee. I did this five or six times as my excitement grew. I was winning!

Then he pulled away, shook his head, and in a slurred voice said: "Nooow you'rrre fffuckin' dead!"

OH SHIT! I thought. This wasn't like in the movies. He was supposed to go down, not get angrier!

We exchanged several blows, and he started to get the better of me. That's when Elmo stepped in, clobbering him after leaving his buddy rolling on the ground holding his face.

Eventually, the guy on the ground was pulled into the safety of the house as partygoers began to spill out the front door to see what was happening. We weren't going to push our luck. Leaving before we were badly outnumbered, we disappeared into the darkness of the alley at the end of the block.

Wow! What a buzz. The rush of adrenaline and testosterone was pulsing through my veins. It lasted maybe twenty minutes, but it left me feeling like I had never felt before: alive, humming, and excited. I became addicted to the violence, the fighting, the domination over another human being at any cost, and the sense of power from the fear that was created. For the first time in my life, I was not on the receiving end of abuse or pain—I was the one doling it out. That was freedom. Once I had experienced the adrenaline rush and excitement that came with my first real taste of violence, it wasn't long before I was all in and fighting almost every weekend. The contrast between school life and weekend life was extreme.

The kids at my preppy school hated me. In response, I donned the mask of not giving a damn, of coming across as totally cold and emotionless. This was a self-defence mechanism, a survival skill.

The truth is, rejection hurt like hell, and to avoid the pain it was necessary for me to control the rejection, to rationalize why these people didn't matter, were fake, posers, or whatever label I could give them to justify the controlled demolition of real and potential relationships. I blew up relationships left and right, the second I got a whiff they were going sideways. Even if inside I felt sadness, guilt, or even grief, outside I displayed a lack of caring, a total absence of remorse, and intentional cruelty.

At first, these internal feelings were powerful and the not-caring mask was awkward; it went against my humanity and my true nature, suppressing my most sensitive inner self. But by donning the mask over and over, the awkwardness went away, the mask became more and more comfortable, and the suppression became more and more automatic. The mask I'd started out wearing only occasionally, when required, became a permanent part of my identity. And when the masks were on and the shields were up, I would've seemed like a sociopath.

Elmo and I would go to the parties thrown by my preppy school-mates (knowing we were not welcome) and skull beers, chugging them in one go, under the glares of preps and jocks as tensions grew to the point where even the hosts called the cops. As we built our own crew (many of the new skinheads were punks we had previously beaten up; Elmo was particularly good at getting them to join the dark side), it wasn't long before we didn't need to hang around other groups to socialize.

One day, when I was walking between classes, I got into a snarly exchange with Rob, a stocky, nuggety, very muscular guy reminiscent of Gimli, the dwarf warrior from the *Lord of the Rings* movies. The exchange resulted in Rob drilling me right in the solar plexus, halting my ability to breathe. I keeled over, gasping for breath, unable to draw in air, and hoping that was the end of it. I had no chance of winning against Rob, and so, afraid of an even greater beating, I didn't hit back. Standing there in fear and cowardice, struggling for air as that sick feeling you get in the stomach when you're winded started to recede, I spat out, "You are a dead man!"

"Whatever," he said, walking away to class, leaving me holding my stomach and cursing him.

Meanwhile, his older brother, who was in grade twelve, had been watching the whole thing go down. He walked up to me real close, stuck his face in mine, and said, "Ha! I beat up skinheads for fun on weekends" and then walked away.

Really? I thought. *We'll see about that.*

When the rest of my crew heard about this claim, the decision was quickly made for everyone to pay a visit to Rob and his brother on the Friday three weeks after the altercation. On Wednesday, I walked into Prince of Wales with an aluminum baseball bat in one hand and my school bag in the other (of course I also had a baseball and glove for plausible deniability). Something was going down. The school with abuzz with rumours of retribution, although no one was supposed to know the appointed day except for a handful of friends. Still, word got out.

Friday rolled around, and the nervous energy of excitement and anticipation was nearly overwhelming. At 2:45 p.m., a stern voice came over the school loudspeaker: "Tony McAleer, come to the principal's office immediately!"

A little unease crept in as I walked into his office and took a seat. Putting on my feigned look of innocence with a dash of smugness, I waited for him to speak.

"Your friends are here," he said.

"What friends?" I replied incredulously.

"Rob and his brother, Richard, have already been taken home by the police. There will be no trouble today."

In my head, I was doing cartwheels over the fact that the threat of our skinhead crew had sent them packing with a police escort, signalling a victory of sorts.

"You can go now," the principal said.

Quickly following his instructions, I rushed to my locker and grabbed the bat and bag. I ran from the side exit of the school across the soccer field toward the twenty or so of my skinhead mates who had shown up. Within a few minutes, there were 150 students standing at the school-side of the residential T-intersection, curiosity clearly the draw. Most were gawkers, certainly not intending to engage in a mass brawl. We knew that if we charged at that crowd, at least half would be terrified and run away.

As we debated what to do, about fifteen Greek guys from the next school over turned up wearing black jeans and black tank tops and started showing off their kickboxing skills. The dynamics had changed and a recalculation was in order.

Moments later, a squad car showed up, followed quickly by another. Without hesitation, most of us handed our weapons to girlfriends or threw them in the bushes. My bat and bag disappeared until the next day.

Again, recalculation. The police presence meant a stalemate. The police told us to move on, as the Greeks had joined the crowd in front of the school. We began to move away from the intersection as an ever-increasing number of police arrived and restored order. We reached the end of the block, turned the corner, and started to walk the short half block to busy Arbutus Street and the bus stop that was around yet another corner. The police were going to make sure we got on the next bus and left the area.

Suddenly, around the corner from the bus stop and behind us (most of us were walking backwards, facing the police and protesting our innocence) came eight East Indian guys, their leader wearing a turban. They were from John Oliver—a high school in the east end with a tough reputation—and they were ready for a fight. Clearly, word had gotten out far beyond my school. In the meantime, four more squad cars arrived. Now we had a problem—or should I say we had multiple issues as we began to close ranks and withdraw. By this time there were eight squad cars and two paddy wagons in attendance. The cops told us to beat it and continued herding us around the corner, right into the East Indians, who were now between us and the bus stop. As we passed the East Indian gang, they challenged us to fight. The police seemed to give them a nod of encouragement, which was not a good sign for us; we figured we would be arrested if we responded in kind.

The leader of the East Indians walked up and took a swing at FiFi, the largest of our group, with brass knuckles; it left a mark on FiFi's face. FiFi backed up, pulled a club from inside his jacket, and struck a blow to the leader's head, which was protected by his turban. After a few reckless swings, the police, at full strength, intervened, and both groups quickly disengaged before anything got too out of hand. The bus arrived shortly thereafter, and we were allowed to leave. Not the outcome we had expected.

After the crazy events of that afternoon, nobody at Prince of Wales ever messed with me again. I was flush with the feeling of being feared and the safety that comes with intimidation. People at my school may not have respected me, but they feared me, which at the time felt better than respect. The twenty skinheads (there were also Chelseas, skinhead girls so nicknamed for their short haircuts) who'd shown up had made an effort to be there for me. Their doing so told me that I mattered, that they cared. The appearance of rival gangs and the heavy law enforcement presence signalled that we were to be taken seriously.

That was my narcissistic perspective at the time anyhow, but the feeling of power could not be ignored.

That day marked a turning point. I'd never felt as powerful or as feared, and it was intoxicating. This was something the punk scene couldn't offer, and that realization essentially put an end to the game of identity tug-of-war I'd been playing. Even though it was a false sense of power, I couldn't resist the accompanying feeling of safety, the feeling of belonging and of acceptance in the skinhead crew. In those years, friendships were formed and solidified over and over through violence and blood. We were bonded by our wounds, and we found acceptance and brotherhood through our scars of rejection, and safety in our loyalty to each other, which was often proven on the street. We had our own rules, our own code to follow to earn each other's respect. Here I also found a way to connect with my father through what I later learned was a false bond: a belief, action, or attribute that we copy to curry favour or to create symmetry with the person in question so that we may be more likable and receive more attention, acceptance, or approval.

The skinhead identity checked many of my father's boxes: Ultra-British and jingoistic. Grew up in Liverpool's Catholic slums. Loved football—the kind you play with your feet, not with your hands. Loved drinking—in particular, English ales. For me, ale wasn't just an alcoholic beverage; it was a passion, a dedication, a lifestyle, and a potential profession. In grade twelve, one of my career choices seriously under consideration was—drumroll, please—brewmaster studying at Edinburgh Polytechnic. My dad would've been so proud.

None of this was conscious, of course. Sure, I was aware of my father's influence on me on an intellectual level, but I was blind to my deep desire and longing for his attention, acceptance, and approval—a yearning I continued to feel for most of my adult life.

My parents, however, hated my new, evolving identity. My dad had spent his entire life trying to escape his working-class origins. "Skinhead" wasn't the outcome they had wanted from a private boarding school education. The punk subculture was creative, rebellious, and, to them, a phase, but the skinhead subculture was a lifestyle. Throw in the Oi! soundtrack and a splash of *A Clockwork Orange* for flair, and that was our identity. To us, the ultraviolence of *A Clockwork Orange* wasn't just a depiction in a book or a movie; it became a lifestyle, and we were the textbook definition of life imitating art, in the bowler hats we sometimes wore, the tattoos, and the canes we carried whose only real purpose was for beating people. Mine concealed a large test tube that could hold seven ounces of hard liquor.

Just about every weekend we went through the same routine of parties and punk shows, alcohol, and fighting. The modern form of skinhead culture was a mix of Oi! music (born out of the punk scene), football hooliganism, and, of course, heavy drinking. Oi! music maintained the working-class roots of a decade earlier but, with its punk sound and energy, became the soundtrack of the football terraces (the standing section in soccer stadiums that working-class people could afford). It was in these spaces that national pride and jingoistic chanting became infused and mixed with extreme nationalism of a political nature. Through these rituals, we proved our loyalty and courage to each other over and over again, even though we often behaved in a most cowardly way. At this point, we wore the badges and trappings of white supremacy without having fully absorbed and internalized the ideology—much like a kid who listens to heavy metal and wears pentagrams but hasn't delved into Satanism or ritualistic magick. At the live shows, punks and skinheads still commingled in a somewhat uneasy truce as skinhead numbers started to grow, and the ultra-nationalism and racism were worn more like a badge than an identity, but that would soon change. Although we were definitely a public nuisance, there was one missing ingredient that kept the knob from being turned to eleven, and kept us from being truly dangerous. That was white power music. White power music would transform us from wearing provocative badges and slogans to internalizing an ideology as identity.

The arrival of a band named Skrewdriver changed everything. Skrewdriver, with its iconic English singer Ian Stuart Donaldson (known as Ian Stuart), didn't always sing racist music; in its early days it opened for bands like Motörhead, the Damned, and the Boomtown Rats. Chiswick Records signed the band in 1976 to cash in on the second wave of punk and the growing skinhead scene inspired by punk band Sham 69. Skrewdriver's music was raw, working class, and violent. It wasn't until the early 1980s that it became influenced heavily by the National Front. As violence between National Front skinheads and anti-racism skinheads (Rock Against Racism, red skins, and other left-leaning fans) was becoming a problem at live shows, bands were asked to declare which side they were on. Some, like Sham 69, denounced racism, whereas Skrewdriver embraced it and was dropped by its label. Ian Stuart re-formed the band and in 1982 released the single "Back with a Bang!"

One cold winter Saturday afternoon, while we were walking across the Georgia Viaduct to Commercial Drive in Vancouver's east end, Elmo handed me his Walkman portable music player and said, "Check this out." He placed the foam-covered earpieces over my head and pressed Play.

From the first drumbeat in the intro to the heavy bass riff that came in just after, I was electrified by the energy, the lyrics, and the vocals of that song. It was more melodic than typical Oi! music, although it maintained the gruffness typical of the genre. The song portrayed skinheads as victims of media slander and police harassment, and in our disempowered state of perceived victimhood, the idea of skinheads restoring their lost honour and coming "back with a bang" seemed right. This format would be followed by the many songs (and indeed narratives) to follow, establish the perceived victimhood and then restore the lost power with violence. This was the best skinhead song I had ever heard. Elmo eventually made me a cassette tape with a recording of Skrewdriver's original album, which I listened to over and over again. In 1983 they released the single "White Power," which would blow the door open on the racist music scene as Oi! and other rock bands released anthems to white power and incitements to racial violence—songs designed purely to shock and offend by using every racial epithet under the sun. Although most record labels turned their backs on white power music, Germany's Rock-O-Rama records had no problem with it, and soon all the racist bands without a label had one.

One cannot underestimate the impact of this kind of music on recruitment, and how it prepared a whole generation of racist skinheads to move from random chaos to politically focused disorder. These young men and women became pre-indoctrinated, primed for introduction to the older, more organized white supremacist organizations. There was also the appeal of the taboo nature of the music, as nobody had dared record lyrics like this before. The music was energized by the politics, and in turn, the politics became energized by the music. Step for step, we were matching the march of skinhead culture in the United Kingdom with that of far-right groups like the NF. But although this music was an essential driver, moving the skinhead scene toward inevitable contact with organized racist and white supremacist groups, it was also disruptive. Not all skinheads were racist, and the appearance of this music marked the beginning of what would become a deep division among skinheads, eventually leading to their total alienation from the punk scene.

At the time of the after-school conflict, our skinhead crew was probably the most cohesive it had ever been, or would be. Some were racist, adopting the fascist National Front beliefs and listening to white power music; others were more traditional skinheads who liked ska and reggae, in the spirit of the movement's origins in 1969. Some were a bit of both—I was into the harder Oi! music then—but we were skinheads first. We slowly became fractured as we no longer listened to the same music together. Nobody was in direct contact with any political groups yet, so the National Front piece was more like part of the uniform. It was the casual, lazy sort of political extremism that a person adopts in order to belong and be accepted—just like there were political stances a person took as part of being a punk but dropped once they grew out of that phase and moved on.

That changed for me when I entered grade twelve. I was taking a heavy academic course load, and some subjects drew more of my interest than others. History class, which covered early-twentieth-century Europe, Weimar Germany, the Third Reich, and World War II, was for me the obvious choice, with my growing fascination with all things far right. This was an opportunity to spend a whole semester studying Adolf Hitler and his forbidden ideology, and it was during this time that I first read *Mein Kampf.* The way my brain works is that when an activity, career, or body of knowledge catches my interest, I go all in. Part of the reason for this is the ego stroke and recognition that comes from knowing more about a subject than anyone else in the room. Combined with a good memory and years spent observing the intellectual banter around my dad's bar, this "all in" tendency really set me up for success (or failure, depending on how you look at it). While earning praise from some, this behaviour sure annoyed the hell out of a great many more. By the time my history class got into Weimar Germany and the rise of the Third Reich, I was well down the rabbit hole.

What began as an effort to be provocative—wearing buttons and pins with swastikas and other white supremacist symbols—led people to start challenging my beliefs. Regularly, I found myself defending my position to people who thought it would be a walk in the park to refute my ignorance. When the skinhead in front of them started quoting the percentage increase in the consumption of meat and butter in Germany in the prewar years as a result of National Socialist economic policy, or the drop in the unemployment rate for those same years, they were often left on the back foot and speechless. Regardless of how smart you are, it's very difficult to debate someone who is completely prepared for the exchange you've just stumbled into.

For me, it didn't stop at winning; there was a need to keep going until the person had been humiliated. Sometimes a person would come up to my buddies and me and start to ridicule or tease us, often with a crowd behind them, cheering them on and laughing. My strategy was to go along in self-deprecation, get the crowd on my side by making fun of myself in a way that was twice as funny. Once I had won over the crowd, they could be turned on the person who'd launched the original insult. There was always ample opportunity to hone my cutting wit and skills of persuasion. Brawn wasn't my first weapon of choice; my intellect and my tongue were, and I was able to talk my way into or out of just about any conflict.

More often than not, my tongue would get us into conflicts in the most provocative way possible. One night, I was drinking and enjoying a punk show with Elmo, FiFi, and a few others at the Pennsylvania Pub, a dive bar on Vancouver's skid row. When the band finished, Elmo and I, semi-drunk and uncomfortable with the silence, stared at the open mic and then at each other. With a nod, we moved in unison toward the small stage. We chanted, "National Front!" and "White Power!" into the mic as the massive crowd began to stir and object. Since we were getting a rise, we continued our provocation until the first chair was hurled in our direction. Game on! We started brawling, with chairs and bottles flying.

As usual, we were outnumbered, but we relied on the fact that we embraced the violence. This was a calculation we would use over and over again. We counted on the fact that 100 percent of our crew was fully committed to the battle, whereas far fewer of the opposition were willing to pay the price. This was the psychological advantage we had when fighting as a group, and we exploited it over and over again. I remember reading a section of *Mein Kampf* in which Hitler describes a political event at a hall in Munich that a group of Communists tried to break up. There were only six or eight SA storm troopers on hand, but they leapt into action like a pack of wolves, fighting so intensely as a group that they beat the much greater number of Communists back and out of the hall. When I read that passage, it immediately resonated with me, and I became more consciously aware of the tactical advantage we could employ. We saw ourselves like that pack of wolves, like those SA storm troopers. This was the fantasy element to our violence that accompanied me/us on the journey from random brawls to the orchestrated violence of ideologues.

Suddenly, the lights from a couple of police cars responding to the melee were shining outside the pub. It was time to leave. I ran toward the exit behind the stage. Pushing through the doors to make my escape into the alleyway, I ran straight into a big burly cop, who grabbed me by my green bomber jacket. Half-drunk, I tried to twist and squirm away, but his grip was unbreakable.

"Where are you going?" he asked.

"Home," I said, in the hope of being released.

"Can I search you?" he asked. It was a formality; he was going to search me no matter how I answered.

His partner started the search, which was fine because my pockets were empty. As I stood there with both arms behind my head, his hand went deeper and deeper into my jacket, and I remembered that there were big holes in the pocket. The officer was now elbow deep.

"What have we here?" the officer queried, as he pulled a throwing star made out of nails from deep inside the lining of my coat.

Damn, I had forgotten about that. Having been found with a weapon while coming out of a bar brawl, I was promptly handcuffed and driven in the paddy wagon the three blocks to the police station.

When the wagon stopped, I was escorted out the back into the alley behind the station and then into an elevator. My mind was racing as the elevator door opened on the third floor and I was led to a counter to be processed. My pockets were emptied and the contents placed in a plastic bag as I answered the questions necessary to fill out my charge sheet.

"How much do you weigh?" the officer asked with a stern gaze.

"I don't know," I replied.

Suddenly, I felt two hands grip me by the ribs just under my armpits and lift me off the floor. "A buck thirty-five," the voice behind me declared, before my feet were returned to the floor. A not-so-subtle reminder that I was now playing a grown-up's game.

When the ritual was finished, they put me in a cell by myself.

I was charged with possession of a prohibited weapon. I was so upset that they put me on suicide watch. I was terrified, thinking my life was over and my future prospects had been dealt a fatal blow, but I certainly wasn't contemplating suicide.

But because my father was a doctor and this was my first offence, a letter from a good lawyer was all it took for me to get a diversion and avoid a record. This scare cooled things down for a bit, but the violence would continue.

One night, four or five of us went down to English Bay to drink. We chose some park benches in the dark near the Aquatic Centre, where the only illlumination came from the moon in the clear sky and what little light came from the street lamps fifty yards away. The Aquatic Centre parking lot was a cruising spot for gay men—which was just why we'd selected our spot in the dark. It was off the beaten track, and with plenty of potential targets. As men walked by we would call them names, throw empty beer cans at them, and utter whatever vulgarity we could think of to provoke them into a response that would invite our escalation to violence. Rarely would we simply attack a stranger for no reason and without warning—there always had to be a cause, even if we had to manufacture it ourselves.

So there we were, throwing out the lures, waiting for a bite, and we finally got one. After the empty can bounced off our target's back, he turned around and told us to fuck off. Well, now we had the disrespect, the provocation for a beating we needed. We leapt to our feet.

"Get him!" someone yelled.

The young man bolted away from us, and we followed in hot pursuit. He was fast, though, and we weren't gaining any ground as we chased him toward the Aquatic Centre and through the parking lot. On the other side of the lot was a construction site. We followed him there, but he disappeared into the darkness of what could only be described as a crawl space about three and a half feet high. We couldn't get at him in the blackness, but we could hear him scrambling and scurrying in the cramped space. After pondering what to do next, we started searching the rough ground for small rocks.

Reminiscent of kids at the lake in summer skipping stones across the water to see whose would go the farthest, we carefully chose our rocks and lined up our shots, listening carefully for any clue as to the young man's position. Throwing my first stone, I listened intently as it skipped along the ground—*clack, clack, clack*—until it hit a concrete wall. I had missed. About every fourth or fifth stone that was thrown, however, generated a howl of pain as the rock struck its mark. With each scream, we celebrated like we were scoring a goal or hitting a home run, until our target finally found a position in the cramped space where he was safe. No longer rewarded by the sounds of terror, we got bored and wandered off in search of new entertainment.

That memory still haunts me, and I carry a healthy shame about what we did, what *I* did, that night. You see, I knew what it felt like to know something terrible was about to happen and there was nothing you could do about it. I knew what it felt like to be trapped and completely powerless. Yet I still put others in that position. I inflicted what I had suffered onto them. As spiritual writer and Franciscan friar Richard Rohr tells us, "If we do not transform our pain, we will most assuredly transmit it." I will never forget the cruelty I committed that night and am horrified to think of the impact it had on that young man's life.

What shocks me most is my state of total disconnection

from my own humanity and the rest of humanity that made possible the events of that evening (and the many, many others that followed).

Somebody asked me once, "How did you lose your humanity?"

"I didn't lose it," I replied. "I traded it for acceptance and approval until there was nothing left."

CHAPTER 4
WHITE PRIDE
WORLDWIDE

THE END OF HIGH school couldn't come soon enough.

After graduation, a friend from my Vancouver College days named Sean and I left for a two-month summer vacation to England and Spain. The trip was completely separate from my skinhead lifestyle, as the two of us never discussed music or politics, but there were still opportunities for me to explore these areas on my own. I arrived in England first and stayed with relatives for a week until Sean arrived. Without delay, I began exploring London in search of any skinhead clothing, vinyl, or iconic souvenirs that would up my status. The first stop was the Last Resort on Petticoat Lane, deep in East London. This store sold everything skinhead related, from Doc Marten boots to Harrington jackets; Crombie, Ben Sherman, and Fred Perry shirts; and T-shirts printed with every skinhead band, image, or logo. The coolest shirt—and one that evaded my search—was the cover for the album *Strength Thru Oi!* featuring the menacing pose of Nicky Crane. The album cover was a play on the Third Reich's Strength Through Joy program, which built seaside spas for workers and their families to enjoy ten thousand at a time, and made the resorts accessible via the autobahns and Volkswagens, or "people's car." Nicky Crane was greatly feared throughout London. He was deeply involved in the British Movement, an ultra-nationalist racist organization; was co-founder, with Ian Stuart, of Blood & Honour, a white power music network that organized concerts and published a magazine; and ran security for Skrewdriver. He would later come out as gay, but he stuck with the neo-Nazi ideology, even trying to organize a much smaller group of gay fascists, and was a steward for London's Pride parade in 1986 while an active skinhead. Crane died from AIDS/HIV-related illnesses in 1993.

My last excursion before Sean arrived took me out of the vibrancy of London on a train travelling south to Croydon, where the National Front had a bookstore. This would be my first contact with organized racism. Everything until this point had been posturing, part of an image and identity expressed through music and drunken ideas. The visit would mark the beginning of a dramatic shift in my life, a pivot to a point where the white supremacist ideology would eventually equal and then supersede my identity as a skinhead.

I entered the shop apprehensively; I'd heard so much of the myth and reality of the feared NF, and I didn't know what to expect. I eagerly took in everything on offer, browsing stickers in bundles of five hundred, and bought copies of *The Servile State* by Hilaire Belloc and *The Camp of the Saints* by Jean Raspail, both of which fed my dark appetite for ideology to support my growing fascist political positions. *The Servile State* was a treatise for a third-way "distributism" that, like National Socialism, was neither capitalist nor socialist. *The Camp of the Saints* was a novel set in the near future when a million of India's poorest commandeer a flotilla of boats and head to France, where their arrival leads to the end of Western civilization. The store had a limited selection of music that included a few singles by Skrewdriver, namely "White Power" and "Voice of Britain," that I immediately added to my purchases.

One of the two men in the shop took an interest in me, especially when he learned I was from Canada (and originally English). We conversed for an hour or so, with me sharing the woes of immigration from the Canadian perspective: the changing neighbourhoods, the increased crime, and the perceived loss of white identity. All of it resonated with my hosts. When it was time to leave, I gathered my illicit bounty in a brown paper bag and hurried to the train. That afternoon was a mixture of nervousness, excitement, danger, curiosity, intrigue, and pride at becoming the first of my crew to make connections with such a forbidden group. With these stories to share upon my return, my ego was doing somersaults.

Sean arrived the next day, and two days later we were on our way to Spain via a flight to Marseille. We revelled in five weeks of total freedom, with no adults. During our adventures I tucked away my skinhead identity—for the most part.

In Barcelona, we stayed at a small pension near the top of La Rambla that cost a mere five dollars a night. Exhausted after our endless partying, Sean went to bed early. I was feeling a bit restless, so I wandered down the four flights of stairs and out of the pension into the hot summer night. La Rambla was always abuzz with activity. I ran across a couple of punk rockers and asked them where the skinheads hung out. Communicating in broken English, they pointed farther down the street and off the beaten track. I headed down La Rambla for a bit, turned left into a residential area, and continued my search before finally coming across Plaça Reial. I realized I wasn't far from the dangerous area the manager of the pension had told us to avoid at all costs. Peering across the dimly lit square, I spied about a dozen guys with short haircuts, jackets, and boots. Nervously, feeling that unique thrill-seeking mix of fear and excitement that had become so normalized, I approached the group and greeted them with a *"Hola! Hablo inglés?"*

This immediately put a halt to their banter, and their shaved heads all turned to stare at me.

"Yes, what do you want?" one of them replied aggressively.

I wasn't dressed like a skinhead, so to them I could have been friend or foe. Scanning their various pins and patches, I tried to ascertain what side of the fence they were on. There were a few symbols I recognized, so I said, "Oi! Oi! Oi! Skrewdriver!"

Their irritated frowns instantly disappeared, and one or two of them started playing air guitar while another began to sing—in the thickest of Spanish accents—the lyrics to "White Power." Their enthusiasm earned them an A for effort.

Halfway across the world from my home, and despite our different languages, this group of guys and I had bonded instantly over white power music. It was as simple as putting a key in a lock and turning it. Just like when I'd walked into the National Front bookstore in Croydon, a shared dedication to racism brought with it not just an ideology but instant friendship and community. The city or country was irrelevant. White Pride Worldwide. This was what made far-right extremist ideology truly dangerous: a loose but linked collection of individuals and groups of varying sizes and levels of organization made up a movement that was basically leaderless, a snake without a head, but united by a common ideology. And the internet would later help to bring them much closer together.

After a lot of handshaking and back patting, I was thirsty for a beer. With the one skin who spoke English, I scampered across the street to the corner store to buy six large bottles of cheap Spanish beer, which we promptly passed around. When those bottles ran dry, we made another trip. Alcohol is another international language of friendship, regardless of politics. After several more rounds, it was time for me to call it a night and head back to the pension to pack before leaving Barcelona the next morning.

Upon my return to Canada, I learned that my parents had enrolled me at the University of Victoria, at the southern tip of Vancouver Island, separated from my friends and from trouble by several hours in a car and a ferry ride. Little did my parents know there was also a skinhead scene in Victoria.

In high school, it had been relatively easy for me to coast along, doing very little work and relying on the strength of my good memory. Cockiness and laziness were two of my many weaknesses, however, and in university this didn't fly. I found myself floundering, and after two years, my time at university came to an end. I left with a degree in fuck-all-ogy.

In the spring of 1987, I was back living at home, working with an investment dealer who was an acquaintance of my dad's, and toning down my skinhead activities for the time being. That would change soon enough.

One day, on the way to drop off a suitcase full of bonds to another investment dealer, I swung by some of my usual outdoor haunts to see if anyone was hanging around. I came across a skinhead I didn't recognize, and we immediately struck up a conversation. Oscar quickly became a close friend, and when he went home to Toronto a few months later, I visited him and got introduced to the skinhead scene there.

I was already somewhat familiar with Toronto skinheads. At the Black Flag show where Elmo and FiFi had sized up my Doc Martens, skinheads from Toronto were present. It was typical for them to make the three-and-a-half-day journey by Greyhound bus to Vancouver—and why not? Vancouver had a lot to offer. A little less than half the size of Toronto, Vancouver (and the West Coast in general) has the mildest winters in the country. Sure, it rains a lot, but there isn't that deep sub-zero cold that goes on for months.

The other huge benefit was that arrest warrants in Ontario weren't enforceable in British Columbia unless they were felony charges.

The Toronto skinhead scene was not only much larger than Vancouver's, but it was also much more mature and well developed. Whereas in Vancouver the skinheads were primarily young and coming out of the punk scene, Toronto had quite a few much older skinheads, many of whom were hardened criminals doing life on the installment plan: six months in or three months out, three months in and six months out—you get the idea. There was also heavier drug use in that community, with everything available from MDA and Valium all the way down to heroin. Out of that maelstrom came some of the hardest and scariest men I have met to this day. Some of them were so unpredictable you had to always be on your toes in case they went on the "turn," where anyone, friend or foe, could become a target of their rage. The Toronto skins had quite a reputation, and they were both feared and respected, especially in Vancouver.

As a result of these cross-Canada exchanges, new friendships and a social network developed through the sharing of music, clothes, and ideas. Toronto was where the older and established far-right parties and organizations were headquartered, and they eventually embraced the energy and vigour of the younger skinheads in what would become a symbiotic relationship. The organized groups offered direction, focus, ideology, and a stronger sense of identity, while the skinheads offered an army of foot soldiers and physical protection. When the old guard was introduced to the growing cadre of young people who had not only embraced white supremacy but were also ready to bleed for it and use violence to defend the white race by any means necessary, the result was explosive.

Courtesy of my mother's travel benefits as an employee of one of Canada's national airlines, I made many trips to Toronto. I would take the red-eye flight from Vancouver late on a Friday night, return home Sunday night, and go back to work Monday morning. Initially, the purpose of these trips was to hang out and explore the huge skinhead scene that everyone kept talking about, but over time the visits became more and more political.

As the skinhead movement in Canada and the United States grew, it began to draw media attention, so it was only a matter of time before it also drew the attention of organized white supremacist groups. When we got word that Canadian white supremacist and politician Paul Fromm would be speaking in Vancouver, my skinhead crew decided to offer ourselves as security for his appearance. This offer was accepted, and providing security would be our principal role in the movement for quite some time. That first organized event opened up a whole new world to me, and was an invitation to go even deeper down the rabbit hole.

Paul Fromm travelled across Canada a couple of times a year speaking against immigration, censorship, and foreign aid. He was part of a loosely connected network representing Canada's far right, from conservatives to more radical elements. The conservatives I refer to here would be known today as alt-light—those who consider themselves to be separate from both mainstream conservatism and the white nationalism of the alt-right. Fromm's political platform came across as alt-light, and this was reflected in his audience of mostly seniors pining for the "good old days." He could always be counted on to supply a new batch of facts, figures, and stories of immigrant crime and failed deportations, not unlike the information currently delivered by Fox News on a nightly basis. For me, he was kind of like a refresher course, and I would load up on his ideological ammunition in order to make my points in arguments. Fromm provided a good public face for the "movement," a nebulous term that would be replaced by the phrases "alt-right" and "alt-light" in the current discourse. There was no coherent body or ideology but rather a collection of loosely aligned interests and politics around what was perceived as the dwindling influence of white people and the loss of a mythologized way of life—many of the same grievances one hears today. While Fromm's conservative demeanour and rhetoric were far more palatable to Joe Public than menacing skinheads wearing swastikas, what made his events dangerous wasn't what he said or the books he sold but who went to see him. These events became the equivalent of a regular business networking meeting, but white power style.

These meetings served an important purpose—recruitment. Fromm was a schoolteacher at the time and wore a business suit, lending an air of respectability to his events. You could bring a grandparent to one and they wouldn't hear anything too extreme for their generation. And new people could be eased gently into the scene, like a frog in a pot of slowly boiling water that cooks to death before realizing what's happening. Attracting older people was a boon because that's where donations came from; money certainly wasn't going to come from skinheads. Once a new member was in and acclimatized, they could then explore the deeper and darker side of the ideology. I was assigned to be on the lookout for those who were a little more than curious and who had a little edge. Nobody becomes Adolf Hitler overnight; there is a learning curve, a progression, a desensitization.

Danger, excitement, and the shock of going to the extremes urged us to engage with more radical elements, and it was during this time that I formed friendships with members of the Aryan Resistance Movement (ARM), former organizers of the BC chapter of the Ku Klux Klan (KKK), and people connected to Aryan Nations in Idaho.

There would be two tracks to my involvement in white supremacist groups: one in Canada that was more mainstream, and another that led me south of the border to the United States and to some of the most extreme elements of the neo-Nazi movement. Skinheads were fairly new to all of this, but since we were plugged into the speaking circuit through Paul Fromm, we got to know both the infamous and less well-known figures of Canada's far right at the time: notorious Holocaust deniers Ernst Zündel and David Irving, and prominent white nationalist leader John Ross Taylor, who was the first to have a racist hotline shut down by the Canadian Human Rights Commission (CHRC), to name a few. My introductions to Don Andrews, leader of the neo-Nazi Nationalist Party of Canada, and Wolfgang Droege, co-founder (with Grant Bristow) of the white supremacist Heritage Front, happened alongside these events. I also met the lawyer who defended most of these individuals and who would later represent me: Douglas Christie.

These extremist leaders soon recognized me as an articulate recruiter and the conduit through which they could interface with the skinheads. Their events became places where we could bring young recruits, both skinhead and non-skinhead, as they were welcoming and not too scary. Whenever a speaker was coming to town, I was entrusted with organizing security. In return, I received attention and recognition for my contribution, which fed directly into my sense of purpose and belonging, as well as my need for acceptance and approval.

CHAPTER 5
ARYAN NATIONS AND WHITE ARYAN RESISTANCE

ON OCTOBER 19, 1987, the financial crisis known as Black Monday hit and the Dow dropped twenty-two percent in a single day. My career in financial services crashed on that day as well, before I even got the opportunity to get off the bottom rung. In the months that followed, it seemed any opportunities for career advancement were dead, and by the spring of 1988, my twenty-year-old patience was all used up. I quit my job to go back to school, but before classes started in the fall, there was much travelling to do.

In 1987, the energized Vancouver skinheads had started to organize politically as we continued to grow in number and swagger. We were given the opportunity to take over the local chapter of the Aryan Resistance Movement, and we promptly moved the PO box from Mission, a small community ninety minutes southeast of Vancouver, to the affluent Kerrisdale neighbourhood where I lived. Our numbers almost doubled to about forty in less than a year, and it wasn't long before we were throwing our weight around. The summer of 1988 would go on record as the most violent ever, as a wave of seemingly spontaneous and out-of-control assaults, vandalism, firebombings, kidnappings, and murder swept through several major cities across North America, all at the hands of skinheads.

In July 1988, through connections I had made at that first Paul Fromm event, I found myself driving down a dusty backcountry road in Coeur d'Alene, Idaho, and pulling up a long dirt driveway before being stopped by two men, one with a Ruger Mini-14 semi-automatic rifle and another with a shotgun. They looked exactly like Hitler's brownshirts, the Nazi Party's original paramilitary, but wore blue shirts instead. They peered inside the car, saw my shaved head, and asked who I was. When I introduced myself, the one leaning in the window said, "Welcome, brother!" before standing back and giving a Nazi salute and a "Hail Victory!"

I drove a little farther, and the trees and bushes parted to reveal a buzz of activity, with dozens of people in all sorts of uniforms and personal dress codes, blue being the most common colour. The armed guard tower caught my attention, as did the church beside it. This was Richard Butler's Church of Jesus Christ–Christian Aryan Nations.

The World Congress of Aryan Nations of 1988, as well as the ones that followed, exposed me to every type of ideology and theology that had at its core the philosophy of white supremacy. Aryan Nations was founded in the 1970s by Richard Butler, a retired aeronautical engineer from California who bought a farm in Idaho and built his church there. Aryan Nations was an arm of the Christian Identity organization Church of Jesus Christ–Christian, a racist, anti-Semitic, and white supremacist interpretation of Christianity that emerged in the United States in the 1920s and '30s. A main tenet of the belief system held white Europeans to be the chosen people and Jews the cursed descendants of Cain, who murdered his brother, Abel. Most of the Christian Identity types at the Congress were older, and some were dressed like Mennonites.

In the weeks before the Congress, I imagined it would be a well-organized paramilitary event. In reality, it was more like a church jamboree, such was the wide range of people there, only with guard towers and assault rifles. There were various members of Klans (contrary to popular belief, the Ku Klux Klan is not a large solitary force but has splintered into dozens of regional and sometimes competing groups of different sizes) and old-school Nazis from the days of George Lincoln Rockwell's American Nazi Party, founded in 1959, wearing brown shirts and swastika armbands. Every major white supremacist faction was represented, but at this Congress, skinheads were present in large numbers for the first time. There was even a group of Christian Identity skinheads from Las Vegas accompanied by sisters and girlfriends who all had blonde hair and brown Nazi uniforms—they were euphemistically referred to as the Brown Skirts. At this predominantly male gathering, there was no shortage of men seeking to get their pictures taken with them (myself included). The Congress also had its fair share of eccentrics and misfits, such as Harold von Braunhut, who, ironically, was born Jewish but dressed like a priest, including the collar, and who was the mail-order marketing genius behind X-ray Specs and Sea-Monkeys. (As a child, I remember ordering Sea-Monkeys from the fantastical ad at the back of a comic book and waiting with excitement for them to arrive. But when I got them, I felt nothing but disappointment at the sight of brine shrimp squiggling about in the fishbowl—all smoke and mirrors.)

The Aryan Nations compound in Idaho introduced me to a whole new world of white supremacist ideas and contacts that were more extreme than anything I'd been exposed to so far. I was taught that black people had lower IQs and were genetically prone to crime; that white civilization was responsible for most of the creativity and invention in the world, and that people living in a civilization they were incapable of creating themselves were doomed to fail. (This was the explanation as to why Indigenous peoples across the world struggled with alcoholism.) Our real hatred, however, was reserved for Jews. We believed that the Aryan man was an existential threat to a Jewish cabal that controlled most of the world through finance, entertainment, and education, and worked in the shadows of the halls of power and government. Such was our threat to them that they would try to undermine us through whatever means they could: mass immigration, race mixing, homosexuality, drugs, and pornography. For the Aryan man to thrive and survive in this world, the Jew, seen as a parasite, had to be removed.

In the mid-1980s, Aryan Nations was ground zero for the white supremacist movement, and out of those years some of the most violent groups would emerge. Knowing this made the movement all the more exciting, dangerous, and attractive to me. During this time, Aryan Nations members were arrested and charged with crimes ranging from conspiracy to kill a judge to full-blown sedition. The latter resulted in a trial in which all twelve accused were acquitted. Aryan Nations was also the crucible from which Robert Matthews and the Order emerged.

Founded by Robert Matthews, the Order, also known as the Silent Brotherhood or the Brüder Schweigen (the German translation of "Silent Brotherhood"), was a paramilitary organization of at least eleven men who dedicated themselves to violence in order to incite a second American revolution. Instead of protests, counter-protests, or street actions, the Order embarked on an underground terrorist campaign that included arson, robbery, counterfeiting, armoured-car heists, and the murder of Jewish talk-radio host Alan Berg. To white power skinheads, the Order was the real deal.

By the mid-1980s, all Order members had been caught and imprisoned except for Robert Matthews, who refused to be taken alive. In December 1984, Matthews' rented house on Whidbey Island, Washington, was surrounded by the FBI. Over the course of several days, SWAT team members made attempts to enter the house, but each time they were repelled by a hail of automatic gunfire. In the end, an incendiary flare set the house on fire and it burned it to the ground. Matthews' charred body was discovered in a bathtub with his Brüder Schweigen medallion, which each member of the Order wore, melted into his chest.

This was the stuff of legend, perceived by young skinheads as a heroic struggle against impossible odds, an example of fearless bravery to which we all aspired. Matthews was a folk hero, a modern-day Robin Hood, and his mythology was eagerly consumed by those, including myself, looking for meaning, purpose, and a role model. At the age of twenty, I declared that I expected to be dead or in jail as a white revolutionary by the age of thirty. Looking back, it is clear that the Order's actions were examples of domestic terrorism, but nobody calls themselves a terrorist or a violent extremist. In the moment, all terrorist groups see themselves as involved in a heroic struggle where any means necessary is justified to remove the perceived oppressor. Everything becomes romanticized by the propaganda.

It was intoxicating and incendiary to be at the Aryan Nations compound, seeing the open display of firearms and meeting the families of Matthews and the men of the Order who were in prison. It made me feel as close as possible to their deeds without actually having been there. Our belief that we were facing a white genocide meant this wasn't so much a struggle for supremacy but for survival. White genocide is the cornerstone narrative of white supremacist groups. It is based on the belief that immigration, multicultural-ism, abortion, and a host of other social policies were designed to eliminate the white race, creating an existential threat that became a call to arms and a justification for any action. White supremacists were inspired by Order member David Lane's infamous Fourteen Words slogan—"We must secure the existence of our people and a future for white children"—and we set out do whatever it took to accomplish that goal.

The Turner Diaries, a novel that greatly inspired Robert Matthews, gave us a blueprint for turning our fantasies into the reality we hoped for. The book is the fictional diary of Earl Turner purportedly discovered in the year 2099, which describes the violent overthrow of the US government 100 years prior by the Organization, a white revolutionary movement, leading to nuclear war and, ultimately, a race war. For us, the highlight of the book was the Day of the Rope, when race traitors were dragged from their houses and hanged on lampposts. Written by William Luther Pierce, founder of the white nationalist organization the National Alliance, under the pseudonym Andrew Macdonald, this book was and is very influential among white supremacists, and has been cited as an inspiration behind many violent and murderous attacks, including the Oklahoma City bombing in 1995 by Timothy McVeigh. This book threw a few more logs on the fire that was already starting to rage and fuelled the fantasies of violence within me and my circle of skinhead friends.

Of all the people I met in the four or five times I travelled to the Aryan Nations compound in Idaho, the one who made the strongest impression was Louis Beam. He was one of the most intense men I had ever known and one of the most powerful, dynamic, and magnetic speakers I'd ever witnessed. Beam wasn't a big man, but he was solid, muscular, and sinewy, with the kind of handshake that could crush your bones. There was fire behind the steely eyes that seemed to see right through anyone who made his acquaintance. He was a Vietnam War vet who seemed like a natural leader. His effect on me was shared by many others, and we would've marched to the gates of hell had he led us. In 1984, Louis Beam had set up the Aryan Nations Liberty Net, the first white supremacist online bulletin board system, becoming one of the first racist leaders to use computers to organize. Technology would become a cornerstone of spreading white supremacist propaganda and remains so to this day. The far right has continued to exploit technology to spread its hateful messages, becoming early adopters of cable access TV, and then the internet and social media.

With the takedown of the Order, the fear of FBI informants, and the sedition trial, Beam kept his distance from any talk or actions that might land him in jail. Instead, he advocated for leaderless resistance, acts that could be undertaken by cells of one, because cells of one can't be infiltrated. Any action was fair game, from non-violent protest and acts of civil disobedience to vandalism, terrorism, and other violent activity. It was during this era that a synagogue in Vancouver was firebombed. Beam created an Aryan points system to allow people to assess the value of potential targets for assassinations; for example, judges and politicians had a much higher value than drug dealers or average people of colour or minorities. Leaderless resistance was a strategy I would promote publicly later on and was a code for encouraging people to do whatever they felt necessary to achieve our goal of a whites-only homeland.

Back in Vancouver, the deeper my involvement in the neo-Nazi scene, the more my relationship with my parents deteriorated. But negative attention is better than no attention, I reasoned. My father had been bombed in England by the Germans during World War II. In hindsight, it makes sense that I would seek to antagonize my father so profoundly by embracing Nazism and idolizing the man who sent those bombs. In the spring of 1989, I attended the first annual Aryan youth conference at the Aryan Nations compound and continued my descent into that world. Held on the 100th anniversary of Hitler's birth, the youth conference was separate from the more general summer Congress and was an attempt by Aryan Nations to reach out specifically to the burgeoning white power skinheads to recruit and organize them.

Not long after, my heated relationship with my father came to a boil. Fed up with my music, my Hitler posters, my non-stop desire to discuss my ideological obsession, and my insistence on going out every night dressed like a fascist Blackshirt from the 1930s, he threw me out of the house. With a garbage bag of belongings in my hand, my parting shot was to put my steel-toed boot through the front door. With no roof and no funds, I applied for welfare and moved into a cockroach-infested hotel on skid row called the St Helen's (coincidentally, the same name as the town in England where my mother was born). Within three weeks, I had landed a great job at a chem lab in North Vancouver doing fire assays for pretty good money.

Fire assays are the process by which mining soil samples are placed in electric or gas ovens. In my social circle (which was now pretty much exclusively white power, as I had isolated myself from everybody else), the gallows humour ran rampant over my choice of career. We used to revel in the irony of a neo-Nazi working with gas ovens. I would even conduct experiments to see how long it would take to reduce a pound of steak to ash—and compare the results to time estimates from the Auschwitz crematoria. Such was the extent of my disconnection from humanity and my emotional numbness that I saw no problem with any of it.

I moved into a house with an older biker named Hal Cooper—a former organizer for David Duke's Ku Klux Klan chapter in British Columbia and a good friend of Wolfgang Droege (or Wolf, as he was known in Toronto). Droege was a German-born Canadian who had returned to Canada after serving three and a half years in a US prison for being part of Operation Red Dog: a plan to invade the tiny island of Dominica with a group of heavily armed Klansmen and install a puppet leader who would give the green light for casinos to be built and run by the Mafia, providing a lucrative revenue stream back to the Klan. The ship's captain got cold feet and called the FBI, who raided the ship while it was at the dock getting ready to leave. Crazy but true!

About a month or two after moving in with Hal, I was getting ready to leave work at six a.m. after a midnight shift when I was approached by a man in the parking lot. He handed me a card indicating that he was with the Canadian Security Intelligence Service, or CSIS, Canada's domestic spy agency, and said they were willing to pay me for ongoing information about the activities around me, in particular if and when something serious was about to go down. They wanted me to be an informant. My immediate response was "I'm not going to be your Judas. You can keep your thirty silver pieces." I took a risk and shared this interaction with Hal the minute I got home, but it was really the only move I could make to maintain his trust.

But now we had a problem: we had drawn the attention of the national authorities, and they would no doubt attempt to recruit someone else from within our circle. We started to pay close attention to those around us for any changes in behaviour or financial resources. A certain amount of paranoia set in, a paranoia that was rampant in the Aryan Nations. The traditional model of organizations with member lists and membership cards was a complete liability, and we assumed that every group had been infiltrated by law enforcement and informants. Aryan Nations offered membership cards, which seemed cool to a neophyte looking to show off to his friends (like

I did). But to a serious cadre of white revolutionaries, membership cards were a non-starter, and the primary reason why I turned down a leadership position heading up the British Columbia chapter of Aryan Nations. After flirting briefly with Christian Identity as an intellectual curiosity, and beginning to see that some people at the Aryan Nations Congress were more interested in dressing up in Nazi costumes than engaging in any meaningful resistance, the most valuable connections and relationships I made in Idaho led me away from Aryan Nations to Southern California and to the infamous Tom Metzger, a strong advocate for leaderless resistance.

In contrast to the Christian Identity of Aryan Nations, Metzger and his White Aryan Resistance (WAR) were atheistic and anti-Christian. Metzger had once held the title of Grand Wizard in California in David Duke's Klan in the 1970s and had run as a Democrat in the forty-third congressional district primary in 1980, winning with a surprising thirty-seven percent of the votes, or 33,000, only to be disavowed by the party and lose heavily to the Republican candidate. He ran in a Senate primary two years later and received 76,000 votes (2.7 percent). His disillusionment with politics led him to form White Aryan Resistance, which ran up and down the West Coast, and a philosophy of "by any means necessary." This is illustrative of a potential danger to consider when excluding people with extremist views from the body politic, as they don't always just go quietly but instead abandon peaceful means of participation.

Metzger fully embraced the ideals of Robert Matthews' Order and mocked organized religion and Christianity mercilessly. His completely irreverent sense of humour resonated with my own, as he didn't pull any punches and enjoyed shocking people. Because of my experiences with Catholic school, I was never comfortable with the Christian Identity of Aryan Nations, and I felt there was far more freedom to move within the moral relativism that accompanied atheism. Metzger heavily promoted *Might Is Right*, a book penned by pseudonymous author Ragnar Redbeard that takes social Darwinism to the extreme, excoriates Christianity and Judaism, and is an ode to power and conquest in the most brutal and in-your-face kind of way. In fact, parts of it were so over the top as to be almost funny, and this perfectly matched Tom Metzger's style and persona. This book was the perfect bible for the growing ranks of young skinheads who required a simple philosophical framework within which to carry out their white resistance. I would read its passages over and over, internalizing the words: "*Vae Victis!* Life to the victor! Woe to the vanquished! In life, the conqueror takes all!"

I had returned to Vancouver from that very first trip to Idaho in the summer of 1988 feeling inspired, along with the few who had joined me. We ramped up our activity and began to expand our local organization, which became the Aryan Resistance Movement. Thanks to our Aryan Nations connections, we were introduced to Women for Aryan Unity, which became our sister organization. Together we would become Canada's largest racist skinhead movement. That summer saw an explosive growth of skinheads across North America and a commensurate increase in skinhead violence as we marched into the streets with new-found swagger.

In Portland, Oregon, on November 13, 1988, a young Ethiopian student named Mulugeta Seraw was beaten to death with a baseball bat by three skinheads in a senseless and vicious murder that grabbed national headlines. It was later revealed that Tom Metzger had dispatched Dave Mazzella, a WAR skin, to recruit skinheads in Portland, where he met Kenneth Murray "Death" Mieske, Kyle Brewster, and Steven Strasser, members of the group East Side White Pride, who murdered Seraw. The Southern Poverty Law Center, the non-profit group that monitors hate groups and extremists in the United States, used that link to Mazzella to file a civil suit for $10 million against Metzger and his White Aryan Resistance. Metzger, who defended himself, eventually lost and was ordered to pay an award of $12.5 million, an amount that ended up bankrupting him. This was the second victory for the Southern Poverty Law Center and its lawyer Maurice Dees using a strategy to seek civil awards from organizations based on the actions of its members.

In 1989, I received a call from John, Tom Metzger's son, asking if I would appear on the *Montel Williams Show* with him. John ran the Aryan Youth Movement, the youth arm of WAR. I accepted the opportunity in a heartbeat, as I was already operating as a spokesman for the white supremacist cause in Vancouver. I had begun doing interviews locally, as whenever a reporter started making inquiries they were funnelled to me. The attention and the growing notoriety fuelled my sense of self-importance. I no longer felt invisible and powerless but was on my way to becoming a total narcissist, in love with the power I exercised through others. Now I could be on a national stage, which meant I could influence—and harm—more people than I ever could have dreamed of affecting with street violence. There would be an audience of millions upon whom I could unleash the most powerful weapon in my arsenal—my voice. I would now have real power.

Arrangements were made and flights booked for me to head to Los Angeles, where the show was taped. I was to be one of six guests, all of us skinheads or neo-Nazis from WAR and Aryan Nations. Wearing all black, steel-toed boots, and a T-shirt with the eagle and swastika logo of the Aryan Resistance Movement over my heart, I took to the stage and put on a brave face; in reality, I was very nervous. Montel was there to, in his words, "shine a light on the cockroaches," whereas we were there to spread our message and justify our activities. Looking at images from that show now, I see a frightened little boy in a grown man's body, trying to turn the tables and make the world frightened of him. But don't let that image disarm you. There is nothing quite so dangerous as a frightened little boy having a temper tantrum in an adult body.

After the show, I spent a few days networking, and I travelled to Fallbrook, California, to meet Tom Metzger and the men who were involved in the infamous brawl on *Geraldo* that resulted in the host's broken nose. Skinheads were starting to get national attention on the talk-show circuit, and that was the program that had everybody talking, friend and foe alike. Skinheads were a new phenomenon to the American and Canadian public, and there was a deep curiosity—and fear—about what their youth and violence represented. For the shows themselves, the great spectacle of the skinheads made for high ratings, and the skinheads who appeared never seemed to disappoint.

From a propaganda and a public relations perspective, however, what was needed was less shock and spectacle and more coherent messaging. On *Montel Williams*, I wore the all-black uniform of a skinhead, but John Metzger wore a suit. John and his father, Tom, always wore suits and were well spoken and eloquent. This was deliberate on their part; they would unabashedly communicate highly radical ideas, ideas that were offensive to many, while looking presentable and refraining from using racial slurs. On TV, they made the unreasonable sound reasonable in order to gain credibility with the viewing public. I appeared on *Montel Williams* with John again two years later, in 1991, along with a woman from the Heritage Front named Elisa Hategan. This time we were all wearing business attire.

The Metzgers' claim to fame (or one of them) was a public-access show called *Race and Reason*. Cable companies had to provide free or very cheap access for community programming, and because they were regulated by the Federal Communications Commission, First Amendment protections applied. These protections meant that cable companies couldn't refuse to air community programming because it was offensive or racist, as it was protected under the doctrine of free speech. In fact, Tom Metzger had the constitutional right to air his show if the cable company offered community access. Every month, the Metzgers would mail a tape of the new episode of *Race and Reason* to people who had "sponsored" the show in their communities, meaning someone had to apply to have the show aired locally. For a cable company to bar *Race and Reason*, they would have to cancel all public-access programming. Some companies chose to cancel the free access altogether rather than air that one program, but most didn't. It was a bold move to take advantage of the public-access programs, and it made effective use of technology at an incredibly low cost. The medium may have changed over the years, but using cheap technological strategies to disseminate propaganda hasn't. Meanwhile, I would soon be ready to deploy some cheap technology of my own.

Over the next two years, things started to shift. After I was laid off from my chem lab job, I started to train as a commercial pilot and took a job in pest control, two activities that left me with enough income and spare time to become even more focused on white supremacist political activities. During this time, I continued to use the airline employee family travel passes (I was still in contact with my mother) to network and build chapters of the Aryan Resistance Movement and Women for Aryan Unity across Canada. It was the Ottawa chapter that organized the first Aryanfest on a property just outside the city that was owned by John Beattie. Beattie had been one of Canada's most prominent racists in the 1960s, when he founded the Canadian Nazi Party, giving new energy to white supremacist activity in the country. Aryanfest had a wedding, tug-of-wars, Viking games, and, as with any skinhead gathering, copious quantities of beer. More than 200 skinheads attended a concert by No Remorse, one of the most extreme white power bands at the time from the United Kingdom.

With the music came visuals: imagery of Vikings and the Third Reich. Viking imagery had been appropriated for the symbolism and propaganda of the Third Reich, but it featured heavily in the cover art of white power music. The Viking mythos of the warrior ideal was used to glorify battle and idealize might is right, total freedom of action, and derision of cowardice. The imagery, ideology, music, and violence conjured powerful emotions, a swirling mix of pride, power, camaraderie, kinship, and bravery that fed into a specific idealized sense of masculinity. In a world where young men were looking to find their place and a sense of who they were, this heady combination laid out a simple yet brutal blueprint of what a man should look like and be rewarded for. This was a model of masculinity that had no space for the soft or the feminine. At these festivals, men played their Viking games and drank like they were on longships, without any understanding of the deeper significance displayed in Viking culture. Few of them experienced any sort of order in their lives and were more interested in fantasizing and clinging to a false masculine ideal than practising a healthy masculine reality. Without this sense of healthy masculinity, young men are more likely to adopt idealized mythological male archetypes that are reinforced by their peers—an echo chamber of false identity. In healthy masculinity, we embrace both the masculine and the feminine aspects: real men cry and aren't afraid to be vulnerable; real men own their shortcomings instead of blaming others. Men who hide behind the shield of bravery are terrified of feeling and having their true selves revealed. Hiding from ourselves is the true cowardice.

Alberta held its own Aryanfest in the town of Provost, which was another hotbed of racism: it was home to Terry Long, leader of the Aryan Nations in Canada. In April 1990, Terry was connected to two skinheads who committed the savage beating of a radio host named Keith Rutherford as retribution for a broadcast in which he exposed an alleged Nazi war criminal. Later that year, Terry needed a computer so that he could connect to various Aryan Nations online bulletin boards; I wanted to upgrade my own computer, so I sold him mine. After setting up his computer, I made the four-hour trip in the back of a pickup truck from his home north to Edmonton, where I met Dan Sims, one of the two skinheads convicted for the Rutherford beating. After partying with Dan's crew for the weekend, and discussing plans and building relationships for future activities and actions, I returned to Vancouver.

At this time, our network was continuing to grow. We had connected to the south with White Aryan Resistance, in the United States, and we were busy rolling out the Aryan Resistance Movement across Canada. WAR and ARM were separate but overlapping groups. We continued meeting with the conservative old guard who still believed in political solutions and didn't support the violence, because we could always find curious young new recruits among their audiences. This same network introduced us to the Heritage Front, founded in 1989 in Toronto by Wolfgang Droege and Grant Bristow (the latter of whom turned out to be a mole for CSIS). The Heritage Front pulled these different factions together into one organization to become the dominant white nationalist group in Canada. The organization was ideologically hard core yet presented a legitimate, even reasonable, appearance.

Here was the dilemma, as I saw it: As skinheads we provoked and attracted too much negative attention; we instigated or inspired violence everywhere we went. I was charged with assault four times, but witnesses wouldn't show up because they were fearful and intimidated, and each time, the charges against me were dismissed. From a purely public relations perspective, it would be difficult to increase our numbers beyond the skinhead community. Aryan Nations was hard core, but I could do without the costume parties, and the old-timers were too soft. Somewhere there had to be a happy medium, a sweet spot. People often said I had a way with words that could make the unreasonable sound reasonable. Leaders of the Heritage Front had this ability too—this was what made them so dangerous.

Here's how it works: Let's start with defining political extremism as a position that less than five percent of the population would support. Now take a position that only one percent of the population would support, put it in a nice wrapper, and deliver it with a silver tongue so that now more than five percent of people would support it. If you can do that, you change where that outer position of extremism lies. That one-percent position has now become the outer edge of normal. When we do this, we incrementally change the location of the middle. When people have no political power, often the only way to move the middle is by moving the extremes. By the same token, people with enormous political capital at their disposal can move the middle at whim, and that in turn moves what is considered the far end of normal to become even more extreme. That is the interplay between mainstream politics and the fringe: they feed off each other.

When Preston Manning gave birth to the conservative Reform Party in the mid-1980s, the leadership of the white power movement saw it as an opportunity to have at least one political party in Canada that would debate open-door immigration policy. Newspaper columnist Doug Collins decided to run for the Reform Party in his local riding of North Vancouver. Collins was a World War II British Army veteran who was captured at Dunkirk and escaped prisoner-of-war camps no fewer than ten times. His racist, anti-immigrant, and anti-Semitic columns were as heavily criticized as they were widely read. Collins won the nomination for his riding, but Preston Manning, wanting no hint of racism in his party, refused to accept his nomination. At around the same time, members of the Heritage Front tried infiltrating the Reform Party in Ontario. Neither attempt worked, but the controversy created a lot of embarrassment for the Reform Party.

Here's where the law of unintended consequences kicks in. White nationalists felt completely excluded from the political process. So we accepted, even embraced, the exclusion, and rejected a peaceful political process to achieve our goals of preserving white "culture" and a white majority in Canada. We felt that democracy didn't apply when it came to matters of immigration and multiculturalism, because these policies were never put to the people and people opposed to them were excluded from the main parties. In our minds, we were forced to be radical; we were forced to start stockpiling weapons in preparation for what we saw as an inevitable violent race conflict.

During this period, the skinhead scene was starting to show the first signs of getting out of control, even by my then-distorted standards. I was beginning to transition away from the overtly intimidating skinhead look, the street violence, and the increasing chaos toward a more mainstream look for wider appeal. Mainstreaming is a tactic of disguising extreme ideology in the camouflage of normality, which applies as much to language and message as it does to appearance and style. The Metzgers taught me that, and the strategy was simple: grow your hair out, don't get tattoos, go to college, join the military, join the police, blend in. The threatening image of the skinhead stood in in the way of the broader public we were trying to appeal to. We needed to be more businesslike than barbarian if we wanted to take our message to a wider audience and attempt to gain more organized political power.

CHAPTER 6
CANADIAN LIBERTY NET

A FEW MONTHS AFTER I returned to Vancouver from my trip to visit with the Aryan Nations skinheads in Alberta, the phone rang. It was Dan Sims asking if I could host two Chelseas who were going to be out in Vancouver for a couple weeks. That was the thing about the skinhead scene in North America—with a phone call you could arrange for a place to stay in just about every city on the continent, and Vancouver was no different. Ten days later, Michelle and her friend arrived. While I did my best to be a good host, they did their best to be great guests, and several times I found myself coming home to cupboards and a fridge stuffed with food and a couple flats of beer. Truly, a match made in heaven. It didn't take long for Michelle and I to become an item. At the end of the two weeks, she stayed and her friend went home.

My mother took an instant disliking to Michelle. Not having been bombed by the Germans during the war, my mother wasn't triggered into the very visceral reaction my father had to my new lifestyle, and she kept our relationship open, even though she despised my increasingly extremist views. Her continued access to me gave her the opportunity speak freely when she didn't approve of my choices—and Michelle definitely fit into that category. I remember driving my mother to the airport for work one afternoon when she gave me the beak. "The beak" was my mother's nickname, as she would peck at me when I was a child in a cross between nagging and a dressing-down from a proper English school headmistress with the values of a bygone era.

"I don't like her. She's going to get pregnant on you and ruin your life," she said in her middle-class English accent. "You are a fool because you don't even see it." Finally, she concluded, with great emphasis, "Make sure you use protection."

"Don't worry, I've got it all covered," I replied confidently.

I grew up without sisters and went to an all-boys Catholic school—what could possibly go wrong? When Michelle told me she was infertile, I thought I'd hit the jackpot, but in reality, I was like a lamb being led to the slaughter. Or this is how I viewed the situation when I was still a frightened little boy who was unable to take responsibility for anything and harboured a deep anger that I directed toward Michelle and, later, women in general.

After about three months, the honeymoon phase of the relationship started to wear off, and we were fighting worse than Sammi and Ronnie, the notorious on-again, off-again couple from the reality TV show *Jersey Shore*. After we broke up for the third time that week, Michelle uttered the words that no twenty-two-year-old boy (God knows I wasn't a man at this age) wants to hear: "I'm pregnant."

I was stunned, like I had been psychologically punched in the gut, and was at a loss for words. My mind was racing, searching for any possible angle to get out of this. Panicked, I ran to the nearest pharmacy, where I purchased a pregnancy test. I waited impatiently while Michelle went to the bathroom. After a couple minutes, she emerged and handed me the test: positive. *It must be faulty*, I thought, and I raced back to the store to pick up another one. After another wait—the same result: positive. I went back to the store several more times to buy different brands, to no avail. I was thinking, hoping, praying that they were somehow faulty.

I wanted so badly for the tests to be wrong, but knowing that Michelle was pregnant put me in a tricky position: if I was serious about saving the white race, there was no other option but to have the baby. This was the white supremacist ideology, going back to the Fourteen Words about securing the existence of white people and a future for white children. The belief was that the Jews were behind abortion in a conspiracy to kill off white babies, and with a declining birth rate among white people, having babies was imperative to further the white race and ensure its continued survial. This narrative also reflects the inherent misogyny of white supremacist ideology in the way it places women on a pedestal while at the same time dehumanizing them by valuing them only for their ability to bear and raise children. The role of women in the movement was very specific. They were worshipped for their ability to have babies but in a very patronizing way, in which they were treated like second-class citizens. The only women who were genuinely respected were the ones who could fight, and they were recognized and valued for their toughness, for their capacity for violence, not for their humanity.

Looking back, I see that the heavy misogyny embedded in the ideology resulted in dysfunctional romantic relationships between people who didn't know how to have a positive connection with themselves or with others. My own relationship was filled with verbal and emotional abuse flowing in both directions. We became targets for each other's anger and pain, and our relationship mirrored so many of those around us.

As the months went on, Michelle was able to conceal the pregnancy with the help of a baggy sweatshirt the odd time that we went to family dinners (which wasn't often, as my family wasn't speaking to me because of their rejection of my white supremacist activities) for holidays like Christmas and Easter, when we had to pretend to play happy family. We were sweating for fear of getting found out. There was no rush to tell my mom, as that would have only invited severe beaking, so we delayed breaking the news as long as possible. Eventually, however, we couldn't put it off any longer. Nervously, I dialled my parents' number, hoping with each ring that no one would pick up, but by the fourth ring, my mom answered.

"Mom, I've got something to tell you," I said.

"Oh no! What now?" she said. I could feel her bracing for bad news, which was typical with my phone calls.

"It's Michelle. She's pregnant."

I could hear my mom starting to lose it, and then her full-force beaking took effect: "You idiot! I told you she would get pregnant! Fucking idiot, you've ruined your life!"

I heard the receiver of the wall-mounted kitchen phone fall and start banging against the wall as my mom walked across the floor in her high heels, cursing. To this day, I don't think I've ever heard so much profanity come out of the mouth of a proper middle-aged Englishwoman. To be fair, she was probably cursing because she knew how much work this child was going to be for her, given the current state of my life. I was in no position to be a responsible father and family man.

Then my dad picked up the handset. "Tony, what's your mother all upset about?"

"It's Michelle. She's pregnant."

He paused. "Are you sure?"

"Oh yeah, I'm sure," I said, as I thought about the size of her belly.

"How far along is she?" he asked. It was the doctor in him.

"Seven and a half."

"Seven and a half months, and you didn't tell us?"

To which I sheepishly replied, "No, no, no, not seven and a half months. Seven and a half minutes. The contractions are seven and a half minutes apart. I'm calling from Saint Paul's Hospital!"

Within an hour my parents would be grandparents, and there would be no more beak. At least not about this.

What happened next was extraordinary. Not more than twenty minutes later, I was in the delivery room with Michelle, amid all the chaos, screaming, and profanity normally associated with your average childbirth, trying to make sense of it all and feeling as useful as a spare tool. As Michelle's huffing and puffing and grunting reached a crescendo, I could see a baby start to emerge. I watched as the nurses stepped in to finish the process, cutting the umbilical cord and wrapping the baby. And then a nurse turned and handed the baby to me. She was a beautiful little girl. I took her into my hands and looked down at her as she waved her tiny clenched fists in the air with her eyes closed and scrunched her face as if she were trying to come to terms with her change in environs.

I was terrified, afraid I was going to do something wrong, worried about not knowing how to hold her properly, as she was so tiny, fragile, and delicate. But as I marvelled at the little human being squirming in my hands, she opened her eyes. At that moment, knowing that my face was the first picture her brain was going to take, I connected to another human being for the first time since ... I couldn't remember when. We were bonded. I felt a tingle start at the top of my scalp, travel down my body, and move out of my feet and into the floor. It was an intense sensation. I only knew one thing: that moment had changed me. I didn't know how or in what way, but I left that delivery room a different person than I'd entered it.

I wish I could say that my daughter's birth meant the end of my involvement with skinheads, neo-Nazis, and white supremacists, but it didn't happen that way. I had too much personal and social capital invested in my identity to let it go. My trajectory deeper into the world of white supremacy had too much momentum. So although something in me started to shift the day my daughter was born, I was still 100 percent dedicated to the white supremacist cause. I continued my path seeking purpose and attention, as well as my transition from skinhead in a bomber jacket and Doc Marten boots to political leader in a suit and tie.

One day, several of us took part in an afternoon of leafleting in downtown Vancouver on the main shopping thoroughfare of Robson Street. Our favourite leaflet featured a drawing of an idealized white family. It was an attempt to invoke the protective instincts parents have for their children and to caution readers about the future in store for white children in a country where they would soon become minorities if they didn't pay attention. We didn't have to use any hard-core language or symbols. However, the events of this particular day provided a great example of how the messenger can reduce the efficacy of the message. People were cringing even before they took the leaflet from our hands. Although the images were fairly innocuous, the experience of receiving that leaflet from a group of skinheads sporting combat boots and Nordic symbols made it seem threatening. For me, this experience brought home the idea that the messenger is just as important as the message, and that the skinhead image was counterproductive to our goal of garnering wider public support.

That same day, I encountered a punk I knew named Fraser, who was a nemesis of mine. A few weeks earlier, he had torn my Aryan Nations necklace from my neck outside a bar and scratched it up. On this particular day, he was selling counterfeit watches outside Eaton's department store. As soon as we saw each other, there was instant hostility, and we exchanged insults. In an act of revenge for the necklace,

I kicked his table of watches over. Realizing he was outnumbered by my skinhead crew, he picked up his goods and took off—only to return twenty minutes later with a club. What happened next was a running battle on foot that went around the corner of Eaton's and up Granville Street. But when Fraser dropped the club, the tables turned, and he backed off and ran away. I picked up the club, put it in a nearby mailbox so that nobody could use it, and took off in the other direction.

Making my way quickly across Georgia Street and into the Hudson's Bay department store, I suddenly realized that three internal security guards were homing in on me. At that point, I knew running was my only option, but I was quickly tackled to the ground. The police showed up and arrested me. However, like the other times I'd been arrested for assault, the charges were dismissed, as some of the witnesses didn't show up.

Several months later, while reading the weekly computer newspaper to keep up on all things technological, I came across an ad for a product in the United States called, appropriately, Big Mouth. Big Mouth was a card that could be slotted into just about any computer and would transform it into a computerized voice messaging centre that operated just like the private branch exchange, or PBX, phone systems that major companies used at the time to offer callers a menu system to reach different departments: "Press 1 for accounting, press 2 for information," for example. But whereas PBX phone systems were expensive, at between $20,000 and $30,000, Big Mouth cost only $350. I immediately ordered one, having recognized the potential to offer not just one message to callers but ten, twenty, fifty, or more, and at a fraction of the cost of traditional technology. Why stand on a corner handing out leaflets when you could let technology do most of the work for you and reach many, many more people?

That was how, in 1991, I came to establish the Canadian Liberty Net

(CLN), which was inspired by Louis Beam's Aryan Nations Liberty Net (an online bulletin board that Aryan Nations leaders and organizers used to communicate with each other) and the success of Tom Metzger's White Aryan Resistance telephone hotline that was set up to disseminate racist information. The first step was for me to take a trip to Victoria to meet with lawyer Douglas Christie. Christie made a career out of defending the indefensible; he represented every major defendant involved in hate speech cases in Canada, including white supremacist John Ross Taylor (whose failed defence by Christie before the Supreme Court in 1990 remains the precedent on which hate speech cases are still argued), Holocaust denier Ernst Zündel (for publishing the book *Did Six Million Really Die?*), and James Keegstra (a schoolteacher who taught Holocaust denial in his classroom). For those on the far right, no matter what circles you travelled in, if you were in legal trouble, you called Doug Christie, otherwise known as the Battling Barrister.

The purpose of my visit was to seek Christie's advice about the legality of our actions and comments in order to avoid criminal charges. Although I tested the capacity of Big Mouth to automatically send outbound messages, Christie deemed this too risky from a legal perspective, so I chose to only handle inbound callers, who had to listen to a disclaimer and press 88 before being allowed to listen to the pre-recorded messages. We advertised the phone number in conservative newsletters and printed thousands of stickers to get the information out. Although Christie made it clear his advice could not keep me out of court, he gave me a rough idea of where the line was drawn; I was determined to walk right up to that line and poke my nose across to the other side. This was a continuation of the same pattern that I'd played out in elementary and high school, provoking teachers to lose their cool while feigning innocence. Only this time, it wouldn't be a teacher I would provoke but the Canadian Human Rights Commission (CHRC).

The CHRC is a federal quasi-judicial organization established in 1977 that has the power to investigate violations of the Canadian Human Rights Act and, if a violation is deemed to have taken place, refer it to the Canadian Human Rights Tribunal for adjudication. At the time, Canada already had criminal law statutes prohibiting hate speech. The criminal code statutes 318 to 320 include the prohibition of "willful promotion of hatred against an identifiable group," which since 2017 includes "any section of the public distinguished by colour, race, religion, ethnic origin or sexual orientation, gender identity or expression, or mental or physical disability." The Human Rights Act extended legislation to specifically target phone lines, and, at that time, Section 13.1 (since repealed in 2013 by the Harper government) made it a discriminatory practice to "communicate telephonically or to cause to be so communicated, repeatedly, in whole or in part by means of the facilities of a telecommunication undertaking within the legislative authority of Parliament, any matter that is likely to expose a person or persons to hatred or contempt by a reason of the fact that that person or those persons are identifiable on the basis of a prohibited ground of discrimination."

With the understanding of these laws in play, we began recording messages for the CLN system using Big Mouth. We started with an introduction that said: "Welcome to the Canadian Liberty Net, Canada's first computer-operated voice-messaging centre to promote cultural and racial awareness amongst white people. If you are upset by the free expression of European cultural and racial awareness, please press 6 on your touchtone phone and do not attempt to enter the Canadian Liberty Net. For those who wish to hear our messages, press 1 on your touchtone phone or press 88 to go to the main menu."

In white power circles, the number eighty-eight is code for "Heil Hitler," as *H* is the eighth letter of the alphabet. The use of symbols in right-wing propaganda is a way to provide cryptic clues as to its true intentions. Another common number used is fourteen, which represents Order member David Lane's Fourteen Words—"We must secure the existence of our people and a future for white children." They're often put together as 1488. The name of the ultraviolent UK-based neo-Nazi terrorist group Combat 18 refers to the first and eighth letters of the alphabet, *A* and *H*, the initials of Adolf Hitler. There are many more such examples.

This opening message was meant to be a disclaimer for legal reasons. The wording was designed to be as tame as possible but also to insinuate themes that would lead the listener to the desired conclusion—the suspicion of Jews. To listeners in the know, the "eighty-eight" left nothing to the imagination and confirmed that we were admirers of Adolf Hitler and Nazism.

We featured a menu of messages from both American and Canadian white supremacist leaders. From the United States we had Tom Metzger from WAR; William Luther Pierce from the National Alliance, who had also authored and published *The Turner Diaries*; and Holocaust denier Fred Leuchter, who was hired by Ernst Zündel for his defence because of his experience building and maintaining execution systems in several US prisons. From Canada, we had messages from Zündel, leaders of the Heritage Front, and later, the wife of Terry Long, the leader of the Aryan Nations in Alberta, while he was on the run from testifying at an Alberta Human Rights Commission public inquiry into the cross burning on his property in 1990. We also had a message featuring the Australian Nationalist Movement, and we were later in contact with the Afrikaner Resistance Movement from South Africa as well as the British Nationalist Party about recording messages for us.

The next menu led listeners to messages about history that were designed to cast doubt over the historical narrative of the genocide of the Jews in the Holocaust during World War II. Why go after the Holocaust? The reason is simple: If someone believes that there is a Jewish conspiracy to control the world, like I did at the time, the argument was that a great deal of their power to control governments and institutions rested on goodwill and sympathy in response to the Jewish suffering at the hands of Nazi Germany. If people could be convinced that they had been lied to or deceived about the tragic events during World War II, then that goodwill could be destroyed. Questioning the truth of the Holocaust was an attempt to reduce and undermine the power we perceived Jews to have. For some Germans, as was the case with Ernst Zündel, it was also about relieving the burden of guilt, shame, and reparations for Germany's role in the Holocaust. Many older Germans shared with me their desire to restore their country's national pride and, in particular, honour to their fathers, who had played various roles in the Third Reich and the Wehrmacht. It seemed they wanted so desperately to remember their fathers as heroes.

There was also a menu of messages titled "Miscellaneous," but they mostly targeted Jews. The one entitled "Masters of Hollywood" inspired fear by insinuating that the entertainment industry is controlled by Jews in order to "shape the fabric of our society" and spread themes of "homosexuality, drugs, pornography, race mixing, and a baseless promotion of guilt about white history." Another message, called "Hollywood Name Changers," listed celebrities who had changed their Jewish-sounding names, and asked, "Why the heavy concentration of name changers involved in the movie industry? Do you think they have something to hide?" before directing listeners to the recording. The last of the anti-Semitic messages was called "Kosher Tax" and suggested consumers were unwittingly being forced to defray the costs of a racket within the food industry in service to Jewish dietary laws that amounted to "hundreds of millions" of dollars in the United States. The message went so far as to list the kosher certification agencies, as well as the names and phone numbers of the rabbis in charge, so that listeners had somewhere to direct their suspicion and rage.

All of these messages were designed with the intention of leading listeners to come to their own conclusion that Jews were up to all kinds of deceptive and nefarious practices. If we had clearly stated this conclusion ourselves, we would probably have been in violation of the Human Rights Act.

While I was building and launching the CLN, I was approaching peak hubris and narcissism. In my arrogance, I believed I was untouchable, too clever and too cocky to get caught. I had by now appeared on the *Montel Williams Show* twice. I would take every TV, radio, or newspaper interview opportunity that came my way. I was starting to get more attention, acceptance, and approval by making myself valuable to the movement through my facility with technology and with language. And I was relishing a greater sense of significance and political power in the more organized white supremacist movement than I had ever gotten from the skinhead scene. In a way, mainstreaming was a way of trading up. Looking back, I realize I was in something like the honeymoon phase of a romantic relationship, when the hormones course through our brains and make us feel like we have found the one, the perfect fit—at the same time as they are preventing us from seeing the flaws, the true reality.

There is nothing anyone could have said or done then that would have convinced me to alter my path. I was, at this point, all in. Looking back, I've come to realize that this embracing of the white supremacist philosophy was not the result of a single moment but rather a slide toward a normalization of the extreme. Once a particular level of extremism is normalized, the next step is possible—and with each step, there is greater access to harder and darker beliefs, propaganda, and conspiracies. A culture of hyper-masculinity is the first step toward utter contempt for effeminate men, and eventually a deeply entrenched homophobia. Bar brawls and street fights can lead to a fascination with weaponry and fantasies of greater violence. A call for immigration reform eventually becomes support for mass deportations, which then morphs into a "by any means necessary" approach. This is where I was: my identity and the ideology were now fully entwined, and I was utterly committed to the white supremacist cause.

CHAPTER 7
CANADIAN HUMAN RIGHTS COMMISSION

BY DECEMBER 1991, THE first complaint about the Canadian Liberty Net had been made to the Canadian Human Rights Commission, and an investigation began. The complaint was initiated by Michael Elterman, spokesman for the Canadian Jewish Congress, Pacific Region; Aziz Khaki, co-founder of the Committee for Racial Justice and former vice-president of the Council of Muslim Communities of Canada; and Charan Gill, founding president of Progressive Intercultural Community Services, all leaders in their respective communities. Following the investigation, the commission authorized a tribunal for May 25, 1992.

In the past, when other hate lines were accused of violating Section 13.1 of the Human Rights Act, the owners of the phone lines usually shut them down voluntarily and a tribunal then followed to determine whether they had, in fact, violated the act. Full of arrogance, we not only kept the line going but also added even more messages. Like I had so many times before, I went into full rebellion mode. Now I had a tangible authority to resist, and my attitude was: game on. I was really in my element here. Sliding defiantly into my role as ringleader, and wrapping that role in racist ideology, I began a game of cat and mouse, setting out to provoke and enrage. My position of complete stubbornness and defiance in refusing to shut down the phone line put the commission in an unusual spot, which led them to seek an injunction in federal court to try to get the phone line shut down before the tribunal.

Meanwhile, on the home front, I cherished my baby daughter,

but my relationship with Michelle was becoming more and more strained. My priorities at the time were me (the narcissist), the movement, my daughter, and then my relationship. While I was focusing on my efforts to mainstream white supremacist politics with a facade of suits and ties, I was still very much connected to the skinhead scene, which continued to grow. But it was the drama swirling around the CLN that stimulated me most. It wasn't long into the new year before the CHRC announced a federal court date to apply for the injunction to get the phone line shut down before the tribunal.

But that wasn't the only announcement in the winter of 1992. Michelle informed me that she was pregnant again. This time, I told my parents right away (I no longer feared the beak), and they began to prepare for a second grandchild. However, I was still grappling with the responsibility of my first child, and still far from being a capable parent; I was shocked and dazed at the news that number two was on the way, and unable to fully comprehend the consequences of my actions. Yet I was also quite excited. My ego kicked in and I fantasized about contributing to the survival of the white race by building my little tribe.

In federal court, I sat in the gallery as the Battling Barrister, Doug Christie, went to work to the block the injunction to shut down the CLN before the CHRC tribunal. Christie argued that granting the injunction would be unjust—akin to putting the cart before the horse and effectively delivering the sentence before the tribunal even convened. The judge disagreed and granted the order: we were to shut the phone line down until a tribunal could render its decision about whether the CLN violated Section 13.1 of the Human Rights Act.

I slid back into rebellion mode. Determined to win, we went back to the drawing board and formulated strategies that would comply with the letter of the judge's instruction but pervert the intent. The solution was simple: move the CLN to the United States. We unplugged the computer from the phone line and replaced it with an answering machine. The recorded message referred to us as the Canadian Liberty Net in Exile and proclaimed that there was no free speech in Canada; if callers wanted to hear what we had to say, they had to call our US number. I drove the computer down to Bellingham, Washington, where I rented a space in the electrical room of a building, and opened the phone line there. I had remote access to the computer, so I could manage the phone messages from back in Vancouver. We thought we were moving the phone line out of the jurisdiction of the CHRC federal court injunction. So far, this game of cat and mouse was pretty fun, and I was completely oblivious to any harm my activities were causing. And even if I had been aware that they were doing harm, I didn't care. In my arrogance, the need to be right, the need to win, trumped all else.

The CHRC tribunal began in May 1992 while the phone line was still running in Bellingham. A week of hearings went by with the matter unresolved, and a new round of hearings was scheduled for August 24, 1992. The CHRC, unhappy with my chicanery in the United States, filed a motion for a civil contempt of court hearing, which was set to proceed on August 26, one floor above the tribunal. The CLN messages now included appeals for legal funds.

All kinds of people from the far right made donations, including Ernst Zündel and other high-profile members. Many of the people I knew didn't have a lot of money, but they sure drank a lot of beer, so throwing Viking keg parties at my family home became my go-to fundraiser, with skinheads coming from as far away as Portland to attend. (When my daughter was born, my parents were in the process of moving to a bigger home and offered to let me rent the house I'd grown up in to raise my family—a generosity I would greatly defile.) My parents later told me that summer was the worst ever in our neighbours' lives.

During one of these parties, we received death threats from anti-racist activists and were expecting the worst in the form of a drive-by shooting. I always stayed relatively sober at these events to run the bar, until I could really let go later on when most people had left. Taking the threat seriously, I had a fully loaded assault rifle, which I had bought legally, ready to go behind the bar, directly underneath where money and drinks changed hands. What I didn't expect was some of the overflow from the house to knock over two sections of the laneway fence and the neighbours to call the police because of the noise. I was pouring drinks when I saw the flashing lights from four police cars in the lane (I had a direct view because there was no longer a fence). Soon, a number of officers charged into the house.

"Who's the owner of this house?" an officer inquired.

Several people pointed to me.

The officer made his way through the drunken crowd to the bar and asked my name, pulling out his notebook. "You live here?" he asked.

"Yeah," I replied.

"We've had noise complaints, so you have to turn things down and keep everybody inside." Police are so polite in affluent neighbourhoods.

I was extremely nervous as the officer stood before me, and I glanced down, aware that my assault rifle was no more than a foot away from his sidearm, separated by half an inch of wood. As calmly as I could muster, I nodded my head in agreement, reached over to the stereo behind me, and turned the volume down to a more acceptable level. Everybody was pretty compliant at this point, except one skinhead in a wheelchair with a broken leg who was chirping at one of the cops. Pieces of the broken fence were picked up out of the lane and leaned against the remaining section, and the cops eventually left. Everybody came inside and the party continued.

It didn't end until the next day and three kegs later. Financially the party was a success, though my parents would soon sell the family home because my activities had turned it into such a source of embarrassment. But this barely registered with me. I was too busy revelling in the acceptance, approval, and respect my exploits with the CLN were garnering. Whatever this investigation had cost me, and was going to cost me, it was worth it. I was getting more attention than ever.

August 24 rolled around and the next round of the tribunal began. Doug Christie went to work cross-examining evidence and witnesses. Rabbis explained kosher food certification and interpreted the supposedly historical messages; linguistic experts shared their expertise about what the words and sentiment of the phone line really meant; and so on.

Not long before the lunch break, my pager started vibrating. Michelle was in labour. I left the hearing, rushed to the elevator, and ran to the hospital six blocks away. Just over an hour later, after a tremendous struggle on Michelle's part, my son was placed in my hands. My heart melted with joy and pride at having a son.

After a little while, though, I abandoned Michelle and the new baby and ran back to the tribunal. My priorities were still movement first, family second—but that was slowly changing.

The second day of the tribunal was pretty much the same as the first. On the third day, August 26, Justice Max Teitelbaum presided over the contempt of court hearing. As I walked into the courtroom that morning, a supporter stopped me and pressed a newspaper clipping into my hands. It was an article indicating that Justice Teitelbaum was the former honorary legal counsel for the Quebec chapter of the Canadian Jewish Congress, which was one of the claimants against me. My heart sank.

During the contempt proceedings, Justice Teitelbaum accused me of fraud for using a false name to set up the phone line (I had set up it up under the name "Derek Peterson"), an accusation for which Christie was able to extract an apology, as technically the deception did not qualify as fraud. Using a false name to obtain services with the aim of not paying for them would have been considered fraud, but this was not the case. However, I quickly developed a sense of how badly this was going for me as the lawyers for the CHRC argued that although the phone line had been moved to Bellingham, outside the jurisdiction of a telecommunications undertaking in Canada, the fact that it could still be heard on a telephone in Canada meant that it was a "flagrant" violation of the injunction. Christie argued that this was free speech and that courts didn't have jurisdiction over a phone line in another country. My argument was that in moving the line to Bellingham, the CLN had gone to great effort and expense to comply with the order, and that this was not a flagrant violation. In the end, I was found guilty of contempt, and the judge ordered a recess for lunch before we returned in the early afternoon for sentencing.

Christie treated me to a fancy buffet lunch at the Hotel Vancouver before we returned for the sentencing hearing. After citing the reasons for his decision, Justice Teitelbaum finally delivered the sentence, the severity of which caught me by surprise: three months in prison, a fine of $5,000 levied against the Canadian Liberty Net, and a personal fine of $2,500.

Inside, I was reeling, but for the sake of the cameras I smiled defiantly as I was handcuffed and led away to the elevator that would take me down to the federal courts holding cell. There I would wait for the sheriff's van to take me to Vancouver Pretrial Centre, the city jail where all criminals are processed before being sent on to their designated correctional facilities. Sitting alone in that holding cell, pondering my fate, I realized that at the very beginning of my infant son's life, only three days in, I wasn't there for him. In putting the white supremacist movement before my children, I was acting just like my dad—the father I had sworn never to be like. Michelle later told me she had cried in her hospital bed as the news came in. When a nurse asked her what was wrong, she pointed at the television as the six o'clock news came on with the story of my sentence, and said, "He's the father." I was released two days later on bail pending appeal, but the epiphany I'd experienced in the cell stayed with me.

During the second week of the tribunal, when Christie claimed that the facts in one of the messages were true, a member of the tribunal told us that "truth is not a defence." It didn't matter if the facts contained in our messages were verifiable; if they exposed individuals or groups to hatred or contempt on a prohibited grounds, they had to be restricted. This was different from slander, libel, and Criminal Code hate speech statutes, wherein truth is considered a defence.

The CHRC tribunal ultimately determined that we had to reduce the CLN to a regular answering machine capable of delivering only a single message, rather than the computer that offered dozens. We also had to keep the language of the messages vague. As a result, our messages became more quietly subversive. We promoted lone wolf action, encouraged people to become more mainstream, and, especially, urged people to join the military. I had been training to become a commerical pilot, and had joined an airborne infantry reserve unit in the Vancouver area in order to receive weapons training; I recommended others take similar steps to further the white supremacist cause without attracting attention.

At this time, another complaint against the CLN was lodged with the CHRC, this time on the basis of sexual orientation because of a homophobic message I had recorded. Although discrimination on the basis of sexual orientation had not been included in the original Human Rights Act, a recent Ontario ruling determined that the list wasn't meant to be exhaustive, and sexual orientation was now formally included. The message earned me a second tribunal, which I also lost.

The CHRC must have spent millions on lawyers, tribunals, injunctions, and appeals—and that was what I bragged about. I claimed that what the CLN had to say was so dangerous the government was willing to spend millions to stop it. In the process, they practically made me a martyr in the eyes of my peers. Being jailed for "free speech" is a label few get to wear, and I exploited it to maximum propaganda effect. At its peak, the CLN was receiving more than 300 calls a day, and there is no doubt that it would never have achieved that level of popularity and interest without the CHRC tribunal and media attention. I remember being in England in 1976 when the Sex Pistols' "God Save the Queen" was released. In order to protect the monarchy, the British government decided to ban the song from radio play; as a result, the song went to number one on the charts. But on the official Top Ten list, the name of every artist and their song was listed, except number one, which was was blanked out. That is the danger with censorship; it creates an enticing mystique around the banned material where there previously was none. When the KKK puts flyers on 100 cars or houses in a community, they do it with the knowledge that those flyers might not help to recruit anybody, but the media reporting it will. The white supremacist movement thrives on conflict and attention, and the media is obliged to report on it, which only helps its cause.

Censorship feels like the right response to make violent far-right groups disappear, yet it is largely ineffective at preventing them from organizing, and it often brings with it unintended consequences. Even Germany, which has some of the most stringent hate speech laws in the world, is now under threat from a resurgence of the far right and the rise of the anti-immigrant Alternative for Germany party. As I see it, the conundrum in trying to stifle the expression or discussion of offensive topics or beliefs is that while they might go out of immediate sight, they don't go away. I think it is better to have these negative social or political elements out in the open where we can deal with them head on by exposing them.

We spun the complaints against the CLN and the rulings of the CHRC as proof that the information we were sharing was valuable and that the powers that be didn't want anyone else to know it. For our supporters, this legitimized and validated our wild conspiracy theories and enhanced not only our credibility but also our reach. The white supremacist movement was gathering momentum, which at the time was being led in Canada by the Heritage Front in Toronto. They also had a phone line and were successful at organizing publicly, holding meetings that attracted crowds in the hundreds, instead of the more typical thirty or forty.

Shortly after the formation of the Heritage Front in 1989, founders Wolfgang Droege and Grant Bristow had rolled into Vancouver on a recruiting mission. When they showed up, pitchers of beer in hand, we skinheads were listening. With the rise of the Heritage Front, it no longer made sense to continue to operate the Aryan Resistance

Movement, as there was much membership overlap and the Heritage Front had all of the momentum, so the group disbanded. Many of the people in our ARM chapters in Ontario and beyond simply joined the Heritage Front. The Heritage Front had recently come back from a meeting in Libya organized by Muammar Gaddafi, who often invited (mostly left-wing) radical groups from all over the world to meet with the Libyans, who would get involved in organizing and funding these groups. Most of the groups were very anti-Israel (which equated to anti-Semitic), and the Heritage Front had been invited on the principle of "the enemy of my enemy is my friend."

At the same time, the skinhead scene was booming with the rise of white power bands everywhere. Surrey, British Columbia, a suburb southeast of Vancouver, was ground zero for skinhead activity in the province, with everything revolving around an old house known as the Hog Bin, which was not a reference to Harley-Davidsons but rather a very derogatory allusion to the women who frequented the place. The leaders of the Surrey crew formed the white power rock band Odin's Law, which grew out of the explosion of white power music in the early to mid-nineties. I organized shows for them to play at; the venues of choice were Scout halls and community centres in out-of-the-way places in Vancouver and Surrey. Even open mic nights at Downtown Eastside bars like the old American Hotel biker hangout became unsuspecting hosts for the band.

The Surrey crew became a force to be reckoned with and developed an autonomy of their own. They aligned themselves with the Northern Hammer skinheads in the United States; the Hammerskin Nation had the reputation of being the largest and most violent skinhead crew on the continent. The Surrey crew's capacity for violence was known to be off the charts. They had a reputation for being out of control and always seemed to be egging each other on to commit the wildest and most extreme acts of disruption and violence. They had no respect for anybody but themselves, and even that was questionable.

Behind the scenes, while trying to appear mainstream, we had begun to quietly purchase weapons and ammunition. Although we spoke peacefully, we were actually preparing for the inevitable race war we were certain would erupt when talking failed. Most of the guns were legal, but some weren't. I recall driving my family south, over the Canada–US border, to the shopping mall in Bellingham to meet a friend who sold me his Franchi SPAS-12 semi-automatic shotgun, which I disassembled and hid inside my daughter's stroller in the trunk of the car before driving back across the border. I was so disconnected from humanity that I was willing to use my child as a shield from law enforcement. The shotgun and the AR-15-style rifle (which I purchased legally in Vancouver, and was the same one I kept under the basement bar) were the pride and joy of my mini arsenal. Everybody in the skinhead crew had their own collection, and we would often go up into the mountains to practise shooting. There was an awful lot of fantasy around the guns, reinforced by the violent white power music, as well as books like *The Turner Diaries* and the imagery of Nazi soldiers, Norse gods, and Viking warriors. The reality was that the majority of us would not have had the balls to pull the trigger, but as recent history tells us, there are extremists out there who are willing to do so. The murders of congregants at synagogues, black churches, and Sikh gurdwaras, and the increasing pace at which these tragic events are occurring, suggests this type of violence has sadly become more normalized.

In response to the rise in momentum of the white supremacist movement across Canada and the United States came a commensurate rise in the resistance to it. Society was awakening to the threat we posed, and organizations sprang up in opposition to us that were just as dedicated to street action as we were. Out of the skinhead scene came SHARP, or Skinheads Against Racial Prejudice, started in New York in 1987; and out of the punk/social justice movement emerged groups like the Anti-Racist Action Network. These groups made it more and more difficult for us to hold meetings or be open on the street without having to face counter-protests or opponents in balaclavas bearing pepper spray. Violence begets violence, and things continued to escalate in a series of tit-for-tat actions. On the streets of Toronto, the brawls were becoming more frequent and more dangerous. Ernst Zündel's house was firebombed in 1995, and the home of Gary Schipper (the voice of the Heritage Front hotline) was trashed by more than 100 anti-racists in 1993 as police looked on. After a concert in Ottawa, George Burdi, lead singer of the white power band RaHoWa (short for racial holy war), and Heritage Front leader Wolfgang Droege led a march to Parliament Hill that was met with a large counter-protest. The racists charged the counter-protesters, who turned and ran; the anti-racists who were caught were beaten, and Burdi was charged and convicted of assaulting activist Alicia Reckzin and sentenced to one year in prison. At appeal, the court "ruled him out as the kicker," but Burdi was found guilty of vicarious liability for having led the charge across the street. Clashes between racists and anti-racists resulted in numerous criminal charges. Along with Burdi, Droege and many others ended up in court, and the convictions were starting to sting.

In Vancouver in the early 1990s, we organized a counter-protest of our own to an anti-racist rally at the art gallery. Out of the alley across the street, a group of skinheads carrying a massive swastika flag marched silently right through the anti-racist crowd. There were also twenty more skinheads and other supporters dressed to blend in with the anti-racist crowd. We were hoping for one of two outcomes: no response or a violent one. No response would mean we had at the very least humiliated them, but we really wanted to incite the crowd to attack the group of skinheads with the flag so that we could use "self-defence" as our excuse to take on our opponents. But the anti-racist crowd was disciplined and peaceful, and nothing untoward took place.

However, anti-racist direct action and counter-protests, as well as enforcement by authorities, made it much more difficult for white supremacists to gather. In 1992, the Heritage Front brought Tom Metzger and his son John to Toronto to speak, but they were picked up by immigration authorities and deported back to California before they could do so.

Collectively, the white power organizations had to use different strategies to get our message out. In February 1993, I advertised an event with Tom Metzger in Vancouver. We promoted a presentation followed by a question-and-answer session. Technically speaking, this was true. But although we gave the impression that Metzger would be there in person, the reality was the opposite.

I had an old fifty-inch projection TV that we had used in 1989 to host an event with British Holocaust denier David Irving when he was also banned from Canada. This was before the internet and video conferencing, so we asked Irving to send us a videotaped presentation that we displayed on the big screen for all to see. Afterwards, using a speakerphone and a PA system, we held a live question-and-answer session. We could host events with banned speakers without them having to enter the country, but we didn't need to tell the media that.

We used misdirection to manipulate the media into a frenzy. They believed that Metzger would be delivering his speech in person. The border was on high alert for him; the Canadian Jewish

Congress suggested I should be arrested for encouraging people to violate Canadian immigration law; and on the day of Metzger's event, people in Vancouver came together to organize what would be the largest anti-racist protest in British Columbia's history, composed of community groups, trade unions, and people of all stripes numbering in the thousands.

That same day, I was deluged with media requests to speak to Metzger. I had faxed the front pages of the two local newspapers to Metzger, who was sitting comfortably at home in Fallbrook, California, and described for him the clear, sunny winter sky and the snow-covered North Shore Mountains. I set my phone up to call forward to his California number and told reporters he was at a safe house. News stations broadcast their conversations with him live, reporting that Metzger was in Vancouver as he described the city and the view.

We used the CLN phone line to promote the event and populate rally points where attendees would gather and then be shuttled to the venue, but at each point we were met by a sizable contingent of anti-racist activists, which definitely discouraged people from attending. We were finally able to shuttle about twenty-four people to the Century Plaza Hotel, while the larger rally of 4,000 to 5,000 swelled only six blocks away at the Vancouver Art Gallery. Using an army of spotters on bikes, the anti-racist activists were scouting every possible meeting location downtown. We were soon discovered, at which point 500 activists broke off from the main rally at the art gallery and headed to the hotel. Before the presentation could start, the police arrived and shut the meeting down, seized our equipment, and told us we had to leave. The only problem with leaving was that there were now 500 angry activists outside the hotel, banging on the windows. We were able to escape out the back into the public parking lot, where we simply got into our cars and drove off into the night without incident. Back at the hotel, however, one of the windows was broken, a hotel employee was injured, and two anti-racist activists were arrested with weapons and Molotov cocktails hidden inside empty cans of Pringles potato chips.

This was a victory for the left, as they had mobilized the community in a way it had never been mobilized before and shut down our meeting.

From my perspective at the time, there were two ways to look at what happened. One was as a defeat, in that we were prevented from holding our event in a very public way, which discouraged us from attempting another for quite some time. The other way was as a wildly successful media stunt that received an incredible amount of coverage for an expenditure of a little more than $100. Either way, that evening marked the end of our public gatherings for a long time.

While all of this was going on, the Canadian Liberty Net had been reduced to a single-line answering machine because of court and CHRC orders. Meanwhile, I waited patiently for the appeals to snake their way to the Supreme Court of Canada, where I both won and lost: the Supreme Court ruled that the federal court didn't have the jursdiction to grant the injunction against the CLN in the first place, but since it was granted, I should have complied. The civil contempt of court charge was upheld and my sentence reduced to time served—the two days I had spent in jail before getting released on bail pending appeal. By this time, the phone line no longer provided the same stimulation and was more of an obligation than anything else. When there was no longer any pressure to drop it and no media paying attention, I shut it down.

CHAPTER 8
DISENGAGEMENT

ALTHOUGH I WAS RECEIVING the most attention I'd ever received while running the Canadian Liberty Net, fighting the Human Rights Commission, and expanding the skinhead scene into the organized white supremacist movement, by the mid-nineties, I had never felt more lonely, empty, and unsatisfied. Everything was going wrong—and it was always someone else's fault.

I was laid off from my lucrative pest control job, and my flight school closed down and embezzled all the student enrollment fees two weeks before I was to take my commercial flight test. Because I had taken out a loan and was no longer in flight school, the bank wanted its money back, and the Canada Revenue Agency disallowed my tuition deduction because the school was now non-existent. In the end, I had no choice but to declare bankruptcy.

I also found myself in a loveless relationship based on need and co-dependency, trying to raise two young children. They were the only source of joy in my life and the only reason to stay. Feelings of total powerlessness permeated my relationship with Michelle, as I felt trapped in a toxic union by the bond of our two children. My love for the children meant that I couldn't, or wouldn't, leave them. And I was consumed by the anger that stemmed from feeling like Michelle had deceived me with regard to the pregnancies and had not given me a choice in the matter. In my state of self-absorption, I never once considered Michelle's circumstances or concerns. Instead, the anger and resentment I felt toward the outside world started to pervade my personal relationships and my interior life.

Drunk on power, the skinhead scene (now mostly based in Surrey) also entered a new phase of dysfunction. Bickering, infighting, jealousies, and ego trips started to take over. Infidelities were rampant and created even more drama.

One Saturday afternoon, I received a phone call asking if I knew anything about a friend sleeping with another person's girlfriend. I knew the people involved and what had happened, but I told the person I wanted nothing to do with it. Two hours later, when I was about six beers into *Hockey Night in Canada*, I heard a knock at the door. Standing there were two of the band members from Odin's Law, asking me the same question I'd been asked on the phone. As they stepped into my front hallway and again demanded the name of the friend in question, my answer was the same. When they once again didn't get the information they were looking for, I suddenly experienced a blue flash—the quite familiar sensation (to me, at least) that comes when you are hit in the head so hard that it shocks the brain. As pain shot through my face, I stumbled backwards to the floor. After weathering a flurry of punches and several kicks, I coughed up the name and the beating stopped. They promptly walked out the door while I turned around, blood dripping out of my mouth, to see my two-and-half-year-old son startled and crying. He had witnessed the whole thing and was traumatized and in need of consoling, which caused my daughter distress as well. My head throbbed with pain while my mouth filled with the familiar metallic taste of blood and my brain tried to process what had happened. I soon realized that two of my upper front teeth were angled inward at forty-five degrees.

Once the shock wore off and the anger kicked in, I went and grabbed an assault rifle, but the perpetrators were gone. I was consumed by the idea of revenge and the desire to drive (drunk, remember) out to Surrey and shoot up the Hog Bin. Fortunately, common sense prevailed, and I made a trip to the hospital instead.

My children calmed down soon after the episode, but it left a lasting impression on me. My mind started to fill with questions about the effect my decisions were starting to have on them. The idea of being dead or in jail as a white revolutionary was fine when I'd been filled with romantic notions of glory as a single twenty-year-old, but what about now? What would that mean for my children? It was one thing to destroy my own life, but was it fair for me to destroy theirs? How much were my choices affecting their quality of life? These questions echoed within me as I began to second-guess my involvement in the white supremacist movement.

The difficulty I had was that so much of my identity was invested in the ideology of white supremacy that I was not yet ready to give it up. The conundrum for anyone who is deeply dedicated to an extremist ideology is that identity and ideology become intertwined. For that reason, facts and logic are mostly ineffective at changing a person's mind. If you attack the ideology, you're also attacking the identity, and all of the ego's defence mechanisms—whether that means lashing out or shutting down—will spring forth to meet the challenge. To change someone's extremist beliefs, ideology and identity must be separated, and the mechanism for that change is not through the head but through the heart.

Having children was utterly transformative. I came to understand that it was safe for me to love them, so I could let my guard down and my heart could start its overdue thaw. Their unconditional love and compassion were infectious and powerful. Young children are incapable of shaming, ridicule, and rejection. They see the humanity inside of us when we are incapable of seeing it ourselves.

The knowledge that my son had watched me get my teeth knocked in planted a seed of doubt and disillusionment. The question was: Would that seed germinate and take root? Time would tell.

In the meantime, desperately unhappy with Michelle and unable to address our co-dependency, I did the one thing that was guaranteed to end our relationship: I took the coward's way out and cheated on her. Not insignificantly, my infidelity involved the woman in our social circle that Michelle hated most.

Several weeks later, that woman called the house and asked for Michelle. As I handed her the phone, I knew deep in my gut that things were going to boil over. Listening to Michelle's side of the argument, my heart was filled with both dread at the drama that was unfolding and relief in the face of impending freedom. As she hung up the phone and confronted me, I thought briefly about denying the infidelity, but I couldn't do it. The time was right to rip off the bandage.

My deception and its disclosure had the desired effect, and Michelle and I separated. The children were two and four. Under our agreed-upon arrangement, they stayed with me four days during the week and with Michelle three days over the weekend. Because Michelle didn't drive, my mother had always been heavily involved in the kids' lives. She drove them to preschool while I worked, partly because she was the only one who could, and partly because I didn't want to spoil their chance to have friends by them being labelled "the kids of that Nazi guy." As my children, they were exposed to the ideology simply by being in my house, but I didn't feel I had the right to force it on them like some other extremist parents did. I thought they could choose their own belief system when the time was right. Even though I had no time for the Catholic Church, I had, at my mother's insistence, allowed the kids to go to catechism and be exposed to religious activities that I hoped would make them good people. The irony is that the skinhead and white power scenes were the last places I wanted my kids to be—especially my daughter, because of the misogynistic views and treatment of women.

Spending more and more time with my children was both a joy and a challenge that required my mother's assistance. Although I was in my late twenties, I was still a boy who had yet to become a man. My mother's help didn't come cheap, however, and although I was her son, she didn't want to be "doing the laundry and looking after that Nazi guy's kids." She made it known that she was doing it for the kids and not me, and began to exert pressure on me to lessen my involvement in the movement. She had tried this before without much success, but now she had leverage. She prayed for me to become a man of integrity. She loved me unconditionally as her son, but my relationship with her was very conditional. Compassion accompanied by healthy boundaries and consequences can be an incredibly powerful force for change. If she was going to help me raise the children, I had to leave the white supremacist movement and its accompanying social circles behind. For the first time, I made a decision that put the interests of somebody else—my children—before my own.

During this period, my children and I formed a very tight little unit, and through them I was able to reintroduce laughter and play into my life, two things that had been missing for a long time. Laughter and joy can indeed be great healers. In the past, play had meant slinking off into the solitary world of video games for distraction and avoidance. Like pictures taken in a haunted house that reveal the same ghostly figure in the background, home videos recorded when my children were young all show me sitting in the corner of the living room by myself playing computer games. But in the two years after Michelle and I separated, the dynamic shifted: my kids were a little older, and now it was just them and me. Things had changed for Michelle. Although white supremacy had brought us together, when our relationship ended, so did Michelle's involvement in the movement. She met and started a relationship with an Australian, and when his visa ran out and he returned to Australia, she followed him. In family court I was awarded interim sole custody, which was never challenged, and I became a full-time single parent. After work, I would pick the kids up from my parents' place and take them home. Most of the time, homework and dinner were already done, so we would hang out, walk around the golf course nearby, and play tag in the school playground. I always chuckled as my son would get as close as a foot away from my daughter before she would fall to the ground feigning an ankle injury, thus avoiding getting tagged "it."

The time I spent with my children was as fun as it was cathartic, and each child brought me unique gifts as I experienced parenting them the way that I had always wanted to be parented myself. My parenting style was the opposite of what I had experienced with my father during my own childhood. I was determined to step out of the intergenerational cycle, and I joyfully participated in their childhood as parent, coach, and playmate. I relished the opportunity to do things I'd always wanted to do as a child but didn't, or couldn't. Buying them a toy that I'd always wanted but didn't get was priceless, even though my son didn't seem to share my passion for his Tonka truck, and I think I spent more time with it than he did. I loved playing with them for hours at the park and introducing them to all my favourite childhood rides at the Pacific National Exhibition summer fair. Parenting in this way was very healing for me, especially for Little Tony, who was still buried deep below the surface. As I was slowly withdrawing from my white supremacist social circle (both out of choice and necessity, as I had to keep a low profile to earn money to support my family as well as receive the help I needed from my mother), my growing loneliness was met with boundless love, acceptance, attention, and approval, but this time in a healthy way. My children were the centre of my world now; this was where I belonged now, and it felt right.

To support my family, I got a new job in pest control. I could no longer organize high-profile events because my new employer knew about my past, as a customer had recognized me from the news and reported to him that he had a Nazi in his employ. I think he let me keep the job because he felt sorry for my children, and not to be generous to me, but in the end, it was easy for me to give up organizing events.

However, with the advent of the internet a whole new world of opportunity arose. White supremacist groups had already been active on various electronic bulletin boards, but Mozilla (the first internet browser, now Firefox) and HTML, the standard language for creating web pages and applications, were a quantum leap forward for spreading propaganda, recruiting, networking, and organizing. George Burdi of RaHoWa had launched Resistance Records in late 1993, and immediately, the idea of using the internet to distribute music electronically popped into my head. Burdi and I had a lot in common: we both came from middle-class families and went to private schools, and we were both articulate and well read. In short, we defied the stereotype of those typically involved in the white supremacist movement. I called him, excited to pitch the idea, but he was having trouble wrapping his brain around it because the technology was so new.

"We don't have the budget to pay you," he said.

"You don't have to pay up front—just give me a cut of the sales," I replied.

He agreed, and I began to work on the website for Resistance Records, which would become one of the earliest white power websites.

The goal was simple: scan the cover of every CD and create a sound file for the best song on the album, as well as a thirty-second clip. This was long before the creation of MP3s, so we had to use the original uncompressed WAV file from the CD. In the days before cable and now wireless internet were available, high speed meant a dial-up connection using a modem and a telephone line. At a file size of one megabyte per minute, it could take more than thirty minutes to download a single song, and that was if you had a really fast modem.

In 1994, if you wanted to open an internet merchant account to sell goods online, you were required to pay a deposit of $10,000. That cost was out of reach for us, so we simply used an unsecured and unencrypted form page to take credit card payments. Within a year, the website was responsible for fifteen percent of the company's record sales. The price of the CD online was twenty dollars, whereas the wholesale price was fifteen dollars; I was paid the difference. As these commissions started to come in every month and then steadily increased, I finally had the financial security to focus on a new career in web design.

At this stage, the internet was wide open. I launched a web design company in 1995, with the idea that if I could find ten more opportunities like the one with Resistance Records, I would be set. I acquired the domain *eatnow.com* and had about thirty restaurants online in order to compete with the Yellow Pages phone directory, which was then still the go-to method for takeout. Then my internet service provider approached me with a deal to join their commercial web services division team to sell and build websites, with a twenty-five-percent equity stake. It was a no-brainer to accept, and with that, I joined the vibrant tech community in Vancouver's Gastown neighbourhood in the lead-up to the late-nineties tech boom. I began to explore this new opportunity and at the same time create websites for factions of the white supremacist movement.

Canadian geologist John Ball approached me about designing a website promoting his platform of Holocaust denial. He was infamous for attempting to discredit aerial photographs from World War II of the Auschwitz-Birkenau concentration and extermination camps by claiming they were doctored. Ball tasked me with building an interactive map of Auschwitz that would offer descriptions and explanations contrary to the historical.

Despite this kind of work, however, George Burdi and I both started distancing ourselves from the movement, but for different reasons. For me, it was my children; for George, it was a spell in prison for the assault of anti-racist protestor Alicia Reckzin. George and I kept in close contact, including while he was in jail. We shared our disillusionment not with white supremacist ideology but with the people and the so-called movement. People were living their lives far from the supposed Aryan ideals of order, cleanliness, honour, and hard work that they professed (my own life included), and the movement was rank with hypocrisy. When people are attracted to violent extremist ideology because of their emotional wounds instead of high ideals, it is easy to see where the disconnect between belief and behaviour begins.

Upon George's release from jail in 1997, a condition of his parole was that he could no longer associate with Resistance Records or its employees. Thus began the process by which Resistance Records was sold to Willis Carto (a far-right American conspiracy theorist and Holocaust denier), and eventually William Luther Pierce of the National Alliance (author of *The Turner Diaries* and messages voiced by Kevin Alfred Strom on the Canadian Liberty Net). The sale of Resistance Records ended the steady revenue stream that had acted as a financial bridge while I built up my web design business. Now I really began to rethink my life.

My children had tipped the scales to become priority number one. I was number two, and the movement was now number three. I started to wonder how I could reconfigure my life to reflect this new order. I call my method of disengagement from the movement "fade to black," which is akin to turning the music at a party down slowly until no one knows that it's gone. I didn't suddenly say, "Hey, screw you guys! I'm outta here!" but rather communicated that I had done my tour of duty and was taking a break. As the movement's drama of petty jealousies, resentments, and betrayals continued to unfurl, I just tiptoed quietly from the room and out the back door.

Why should I be like Don Quixote tilting at windmills? I thought to myself. *Why should I fight for a bunch of white people who don't give a damn whether I live or die?* If I really wanted to fight for the white race, then my focus should be on helping my two children survive and thrive. "We must secure the existence of our people and a future for white children." This was how my ego rationalized leaving the movement behind while staying true to the foundational white supremacist tenet of the Fourteen Words. There was no way that my ego was going to let go of my identity as a white supremacist, and when I left the movement, I left with my ideology intact. I wasn't going to be a traitor, or one of those guys who goes on the high-school speaking circuit confessing his sins. (Oh, the irony.)

The process of disengagement is the first step in leaving an extremist group, and involves leaving behind the social circles and the activities but not necessarily the ideology. This is considered a harm-reduction strategy, as a person is better off out of the movement, even if they hold on to the ideology. I call the place I found myself in "the void." When someone leaves an extremist group, they enter a significant period in which they no longer have a social group or a social identity. They are between two distant shores, and they must leave one behind fully if they're going to arrive successfully on the other. Without fully abandoning the first shore, they can never completely reach their destination—their humanity.

Loneliness is one of the difficult parts of disengagement. When someone joins a violent extremist group, they excommunicate themselves from friends, family, and society in order to get the perceived acceptance, approval, and attention they are so desperately seeking. When that person leaves the extremist group behind, they have to repeat that process all over again, except their original friends and family aren't waiting with open arms to welcome them back, and nor is society. The trust of those individuals was betrayed when the relationships were orignally broken. That trust must be earned back, and it certainly doesn't happen overnight. In fact, it takes years.

When I was working in the tech sector in Vancouver's Gastown, I started frequenting an Irish bar that had recently opened in the area, and I got to know the owner, barman, and other patrons quite well. In those early days of the bar's life, several of us would often stay behind for a "shut-in." This was when selected patrons could stay behind after closing time and continue drinking into the wee hours of the morning with the curtains drawn tightly shut. One Thursday afternoon after leaving the office, I popped by for a pint of the black stuff before going home. The owner greeted me as usual, and then pulled me aside and asked if he could have a word.

"What's up?" I asked.

The owner replied, "Tony, I have got a bit of a problem here. There are about twenty people who say they won't come in my restaurant if you are here. They have told me who you are."

My heart sank, and I fought back tears. An entirely new social circle disintegrated in an instant. In the past, I'd occasionally had to leave parties when someone recognized me. But this hurt far, far more because of the time I had invested in these new relationships. There was no anger, just sadness and some shame. I didn't set foot in that bar for a very long time, out of respect for the owner. There was no blaming anyone else for this, and I accepted that it was the price I had to pay for the things I had done, though the loneliness was hard to swallow and didn't leave me for some time.

Not surprisingly, loneliness poses the greatest risk to someone trying to leave an extremist group. Faced with a pain that seems far greater than the pain of the dysfunction they left behind, a disengaging extremist can be tempted to return to their past life. Believe me, I was. Often, I would return home from the bar alone in a state of melancholy, and I would listen to the old music from my skinhead days and reflect on those times through a rose-coloured lens of camaraderie and belonging. Through the music, I could rejoin the movement—but in spirit only, as I was still set on leaving it all behind.

My determination to leave the white supremacist movement was cemented by a realization I had while watching *American History X*. Released in 1998, the film is about a neo-Nazi who goes to prison for killing two black youths but vows to change his ways to prevent his younger brother from going down the same path. The film departed from the familiar Hollywood stereotype of racists as easy-to-despise cardboard characters and was well researched and realistic in its depiction of white supremacist individuals and groups. Some of the characters were more recognizable as being taken from real life than others, with Edward Norton's Derek Vinyard being a blend of a few real-life white supremacists. Stacy Keach's character, Cameron Alexander, was clearly based on Tom Metzger, and the coincidence of the heavyset skinhead who worked in pest control was not lost on me.

This film continues to have a profound impact on me, and there are many lessons we can take from it today, such as the futility of arguing with a white supremacist (because behind the ideology is often a legitimate grievance, albeit one that is mixed with a very flawed solution), as well as the power of compassion, combined with healthy boundaries and consequences, to effect change.

The most powerful lesson came to me when I watched the film on video at home for the first time. When the African American history teacher Dr Sweeney visits Derek in the prison infirmary after Derek is raped by other Aryan prison gang members, he asks a very simple question: "Has anything you've done made your life better?" Derek responds by sobbing and shaking his lowered head. The hypocrisy and betrayal of the neo-Nazis depicted in the film resonated with me. And in that moment, I asked myself the same question and came to the same conclusion. I too was overwhelmed by tears, sobbing, and a sense of deep sadness. Indeed, nothing that I had done for the white supremacist cause had made my life better. In fact, I realized, with the help of some of the perspective gained from my children, it had actually made it worse. Moreover, it had made things worse for everyone within my sphere of influence.

However, I was still too self-obsessed to see or recognize the damage I had done to the communities and individuals who were the undeserving targets of my wrath. That would come later, with the assistance of somebody with the skill set to evoke that awareness.

The epiphany I had while watching the film cemented my decision to leave the movement and dispelled any doubt I was feeling about not turning back. Consciously and deliberately, I set out to break many of the taboos that would make it impossible for me to return.

As a full-time parent, I had little opportunity to go out, so my evenings were mostly spent online, playing video games and trolling or flirting in chat rooms, which led me to connect with one particular twenty-three-year-old woman. Flirting and chatting grew into long late-night phone calls, and I soon learned her name and that she was Punjabi. I experienced some uncomfortable internal dialogue about transgressing one of the primary rules of the movement—no race mixing. If I were to pursue this relationship, I would be considered a race traitor, one of the highest forms of disgrace in the movement to which I had dedicated so much of my adult life. Despite this, I was determined to explore this relationship (the calls were becoming increasingly sexual in nature) and take it to its obvious conclusion: meeting in person. Pushing myself well beyond my comfort levels, I waited nervously for her arrival at our first face-to-face meeting (we hadn't even exchanged photos). The nervousness, the taboo, the lust, and the mystery all culminated in an intoxicating brew that filled me with a reluctant excitement that was impossible to resist. When, at last, I heard the knock at the door and opened it, the chemistry was instantaneous. Through online chat and the telephone, the sexual tension that had developed sight unseen was powerful. It never ceases to amaze me how much surface appearances can affect our judgments and how much richer the information we take in is when we have only our imaginations at our disposal. I was taken aback by the radiant beauty before me that I wouldn't have even recognized a few years ago, when I only saw beauty in white women.

Our relationship continued for more than a year, but we never went out on dates or in public, and she never visited me while my kids were awake. We spent a lot of time together, and in hindsight, I know we were both breaking taboos. She told me she was was expected to marry a man from her Punjabi community someday, and I was aware of my own feeling of shame that arose at the beginning of the relationship. This dissipated over time, though, as my old conditioning slowly dissolved; I was consciously deprogramming myself. I was now a race traitor, and I was okay with that.

This wasn't the only relationship in which taboos were broken. I decided to exchange my equity in the web services business for the rights to source code essential for the development of a multilingual real estate software system venture and joined forces with a new business partner named Jack Tang. Jack told me his father had been governor of Yunnan province in southwestern China and had an extensive network of contacts in the government in Beijing. Again, opening myself up to new opportunities and experiences, I spent a lot of time with Jack. He taught me Mandarin (at least enough to haggle in the markets of Beijing when we eventually went to China), and we developed a great friendship. It was at the airport on my way back from one of these trips to China that I would be pulled into secondary inspection by customs officials and questioned not about my voyage but, because of my identity as a known skinhead, about a crime that would rock the city of Vancouver: the murder of Nirmal Singh Gill.

In the early morning of January 3, 1998, sixty-five-year-old Nirmal Singh Gill arrived at the Guru Nanak Sikh temple in Surrey, British Columbia, to prepare for the morning worship. He came across five skinheads vandalizing cars in the parking lot on the way home from a boozefest nearby, the kind I used to revel in. Nirmal confronted the men and attempted to chase them off, but they didn't leave. Instead, they turned on him and, with their heavy boots, savagely stomped him to death in the parking lot. As they were beating him, one of them tried to take his bracelet, which Nirmal fiercely resisted. The material value of the iron bracelet was negligible, but the religious significance was enormous, and he died fighting to hang on to his *kara*, a reminder that God has no beginning, middle, or end: one of the five sacred symbols of Sikhism.

Initially, suspicion fell upon the Sikh community itself, as there had been previous violent conflicts between moderate and fundamentalist Sikhs. Skinheads weren't the suspects, and they might have gotten away with the murder if they'd kept their mouths shut. But they were overheard bragging about it, and word eventually made its way to the police department. A judge would later describe them as "moronic braggarts."

Once the perpetrators were identified, undercover police posing as bikers willing to finance a race war secured the confessions of some of the attackers. Three months after the murder of Nirmal Singh Gill, the five skinheads were arrested. The youngest was seventeen and bragged he was the first to stomp Gill. There was discussion of a mass murder plot against Sikh schoolchildren and a vow to blow up a Sikh temple if they were ever fingered for Gill's murder. One of the accused even said, "Kill one Sikh, you are a murderer; kill many, you are a conqueror; and kill them all, you are a god."

I was critical of the murder then, but not out of any sense of morality. The criticism was that the killing was a tactical error in the white struggle; it invited all kinds of scrutiny and heat over what I viewed as a meaningless target. How did it advance the cause? I processed this event as data stripped of any human connection and context. Even so, the murder was the end of my social relationship with skinheads, as the whole scene was now so clearly out of control.

CHAPTER 9
RADICAL COMPASSION

ALTHOUGH MY PHYSICAL DISENGAGEMENT from the white supremacist movement was complete by the early 2000s, I was still very unaware of how limited the process of disengagement actually is. Disengagement is only the first step on the road to rehabilitation; it is a form of harm reduction at a very basic level, something that hardly seems worth celebrating: *Oh great, Tony, you stopped being an asshole! Good job!*

Now it was time for the real work to begin.

In 2004, I began yet another new career and returned to financial services, where I wasted no time in throwing myself into my work and satisfying my craving for acknowledgment, recognition, and achievement, albeit in a healthier way. I soon became one of the top new advisors in the firm. I was the guy who always asked complicated questions during presentations to demonstrate to the rest of the room how smart I was, and I had no problem fitting into the drinking culture that existed then.

I kept in touch with George Burdi as he continued to drift out of the movement. He married a Hindu woman of Indian descent and began to immerse himself in Eastern philosophy. The intellectual and spiritual discoveries he shared awakened a curiosity within me. At the same time, my mother (who had converted to Catholicism) was sharing her brand of spirituality with me over long walks and talks together, as she could see a crack opening in the door. I had no intention of going back to the Catholic Church as an institution, but I was curious about some of the spiritual components that were shared by other faiths. I eventually bought my mother the book *Without Buddha I Could Not Be a Christian* by Paul Knitter, an examination of Christianity through a Buddhist lens and rediscovery of faith. To be clear, I had no time for organized religion, but for a long time I questioned my former atheism and often wondered, *Is this all there is?* At this point in my life—when I had physically removed myself from the scene and my life had started to change for the better—everything was open for debate.

George, like me, could be quite persuasive. We had many discussions about his experience with, and the benefits of, meditation, which I had never tried. He suggested we attend a meditation retreat together. I agreed and in preparation read a few books, the best of which was *The Art of Living: Vipassana Meditation as Taught by S.N. Goenka*, which is a very accessible introduction to Buddhism and Vipassana meditation. I also began to practise yoga, as the thought of sitting cross-legged for extended periods was daunting considering my inflexibility.

Six months later, George and I drove up to a meditation centre in Merritt, a city three and a half hours northeast of Vancouver in the interior of British Columbia. My first experience of meditation was going to be a ten-day Vipassana retreat. Ten days of no reading, no writing, no talking—just meditating. There were short periods of instruction in the Vipassana method each day, but the majority of the time was spent meditating in silence. And so, the person who normally couldn't sit still and had been born with the Irish gift of the gab set out to achieve what might be, I worried in the back of my mind, an impossible task. But even though the retreat was one of the most difficult experiences of my life, it was also one of the most profound.

The Vipassana technique starts with simply observing one's breath going in and out of one's nose, which sounds like an easy task but is actually somewhat difficult in practice because the mind, like a crazed monkey, will come and grab your attention. Four days passed before my monkey mind gave up the battle for my attention and the internal chatter stopped.

The theory behind the practice goes something like this: just about all of our experiences create conditioning, and we are constantly piling on new layers of conditioning as we experience life. In a setting of essentially sensory deprivation, where we stop adding new layers, the process reverses itself, and our old conditioning rises to the surface and manifests itself in the body through different sensations. The technique involves scanning different parts of the body to observe these sensations that arise and are released.

Our consciousness is like a microscope, and the more time I spent observing my body, the more I focused, and the more sensitive it became, like moving to higher and higher levels of magnification. By day four, I could feel individual hair follicles as I observed my breath going in and out of my nose.

But about halfway through day six, my chest filled with anxiety and my stomach started churning in a flux between yearning and despair, like I was a lovesick fifteen-year-old who had just been dumped for the very first time. My right arm and upper torso descended into uncontrollable trembling, which was frightening and confusing. Something powerful was being released, but I didn't yet know what.

During days seven and eight, I was able to calmly observe my body and feel the prana, or life energy, flowing through it. Through meditation, we are supposed to be able to observe the mind-body connection; in Eastern philosophy, the mind is not restricted to the head but exists throughout the body.

After ten days, the retreat ended. On the way home, I called both my mother as well as a good friend to try to explain the experience, but how do you describe a mystical experience to someone who perhaps has never had one? I had gained this expansive level of understanding and knowingness in my consciousness, and I was trying to force it out through the tiny aperture at the front of my face called a mouth. Imagine having a completely rich experience that engaged all five senses and trying to explain that experience through the use of only one of those senses. You simply can't do it justice. I soon realized that trying to describe something so profound was beyond the limitations of language, and I sounded like a gibbering madman, so I stopped trying.

The biggest takeaway from the retreat for me was that I was able to experience myself through an empty mind for the first time. The understanding that I was not the sum of my thoughts was profound. I had spent most of my life enslaved by the constant chatter, my conditioning, the little voice in my head. We are not that voice, I discovered; we are so much more.

If I was not my thoughts, then who was I? This depth of inquiry followed me out of the retreat and spurred a quest for discovery that would take me on a journey inward. Until then, I had only ever interacted with, explored, or queried the world outside of me; now I was about to embark on an internal voyage of discovery. My life thus far had been geared toward running in a direction opposite to the one I was about to travel.

In 2005, about a month or two after the retreat, I was still processing the experience—to the point where a friend said that I sometimes went "away with the faeries" for brief periods. Then I watched *What the Bleep Do We Know!?*, a film that explores the spiritual connection between quantum physics and consciousness, along the central theme of "We create our own reality." I found the intersection of science and spirituality fascinating. Shortly afterwards, in this period of curiosity and exploration of new ideas and different ways of looking at things, I attended an introductory lecture about getting out of your own way and achieving success. It was here that I signed up for a weekend workshop facilitated by someone named Dõv Baron.

Immediately, I felt drawn to Dõv. He was about ten years older than me, from Manchester, an industrial city in the northwest of England similar to my hometown of Liverpool, and we bonded over a shared quirky British sense of humour and a love of Monty Python. His workshops were taught from the intersection point of quantum physics, metaphysics (or spirituality), and psychology. They were designed to help people change their inner dialogue and step out of their conditioning to take control of their lives: to move from an unconscious life to a conscious one, to become awakened to the true nature of reality and who we are.

My mind was resistant to what I thought of as the woo-woo side of things, but I found myself deeply interested in the quantum physics explanations for the spiritual. The psychology component of the workshop was about healing early traumas and wounds that had cast a shadow over your life. "Don't let your past put your future in a headlock" was a quote that really resonated with me.

As I delved deeper into the teachings from Dõv's workshop, my life began to improve in remarkable ways. In the beginning, my focus was on my career and financial success, but it didn't take long for it to shift to something much, much deeper. About ten months after I met Dõv, my friend Damien, who had introduced us, handed me an envelope for my birthday. Excitedly, I tore it open and pulled out a gift certificate for an introductory one-on-one counselling session with Dõv. *Oh, great,* I thought to myself. *Best present ever. Who doesn't want therapy for their birthday?* But I had just begun to scratch the surface of my self-exploration, and I was curious to discover what lay beneath. So a few days later, I called to make an appointment and then went to my very first counselling session.

I sat down on the couch across from Dōv and we engaged in a few minutes of small talk before we got into it. He asked me about my childhood. I gave him all the reasons why I was angry: at my dad for not being there and for his betrayal, at my school for the beatings. But I paused when it came to the next part of my story: about becoming a skinhead, a neo-Nazi, the violence, and all of the harm I had done with my tongue and with my pen. I froze, unable to proceed. A million thoughts of shame and guilt mixed with a myriad of fearful calculations—*What if? Should I tell him?*—and I hesitated to speak. I was afraid to tell him the whole truth about who I was and what I had done. This was a relationship, a friendship, that I had only begun to enjoy and value. When people found out about my past, the relationship usually ended, and I was terrified of losing this one.

"Just spit it out," he said. "It's okay, mate. It is safe here."

Despite his reassurances, I was still paralyzed by the dread of judgment and loss. Finally, with great fear and trepidation, I allowed the floodgates to open and started blurting out the *Reader's Digest* version of my story.

But the more I told him, the more he smiled; and the more he smiled, the more I became annoyed. I thought to myself, *Why is he smiling? Here I am baring my soul, and this guy thinks I'm hilarious.*

Irritated, I asked him, "What's so funny?"

Dōv leaned over the coffee table with a grin from ear to ear and said, "You know I was born Jewish, right?"

Of course he was. The irony of that wasn't lost on me as I began to sink into the couch, my cheeks burning with deep shame. This was a person whom I considered a friend, a person who wanted the best for me, wanted to heal me, and here I was, sitting across the coffee table from him, knowing that I had once advocated for the annihilation of him and his people.

While I was trying to process the implications of this moment, Dōv spoke. "This is what you did. It is not who you are." Then he pointed at me. "I see you. I see the little boy inside of you. I see Little Tony."

No sooner had those words left his lips than I broke down sobbing. In that moment, when I felt so worthless, I was overcome by his acknowledgment of the humanity within me, even knowing the harm I'd done to his people. When I felt I deserved it least, I could feel the warmth of his compassion. If this man could love me, there was no reason why I couldn't learn to love myself. Compassion from somebody we don't feel we deserve it from, especially from someone who comes from a community we have dehumanized, is incredibly powerful. (But I am not suggesting for a minute that it is the responsibility of members of marginalized communities to take this on.)

If empathy is feeling what somebody else is feeling in their suffering, then compassion is empathy plus action—the desire to alleviate the suffering of others. Empathy + Action = Compassion. Radical compassion goes a step further and takes us outside of our comfort zone: having compassion for people we don't like, being willing to take a risk or experience some discomfort, or finally, wanting to go even further and engage in social change through our compassion, to change the environment that is the source of the suffering we witness in the world. Radical compassion starts with compassion for the self, which amplifies our capacity to serve others. To face our fears and our pain, to push through the discomfort of vulnerability, is one of the most radical acts we can undertake. The more I can understand myself, the more I can understand others. The more I can feel within myself, the more I can feel others. And the more I can have compassion for myself, the more I can have compassion for others. The journey inward to know ourselves is crucial to radical compassion, as it provides the necessary balance to truly effect change. If we have compassion for others and not ourselves, then it is not compassion but about ego, about being seen to be compassionate. And if we have compassion for ourselves and no one else, then it is not compassion but narcissism. Compassion within and compassion without—the two in balance—is a truly powerful combination, a place from which our fear and judgment can transform into understanding and healing. That which we don't transform, we transmit.

That moment when I received radical compassion from my mentor Dōv marked the beginning of an incredible journey deep into the darkest reaches of my subconscious—a journey toward the fear, toward the wounds, toward the pain that had cast their shadows across my life until then, the pain that I had been running away from my entire life. In both one-on-one and group counselling sessions, I spent more than 1,000 hours in self-discovery, uncovering and healing these wounds, and observing the same process in others. Rewriting the belief systems at the core of my being and pulling off the layers of masks to learn who the authentic me was and to reconnect to my humanity and to Little Tony. Understanding how I ended up in the dark woods, and how I eventually found my way out so that others could learn from my journey.

The best way to describe my previous state of unfeeling is as profound emotional numbness, an emotionally transmitted disease, a condition (which is also contagious) that started gradually and progressed to eventually afflict my entire being to the point where my very soul was disfigured. As a young boy, I was highly sensitive, but I simply wasn't in a place where it was safe to be that way. Bit by bit, I shut my sensitivities down. The internal effects of emotional numbness are invisible to the naked eye. A person might display their numbness through their choices and actions. They might appear clumsy in social situations that require emotional intelligence and interpersonal skills. The emotional wounds at the core of my being shaped, changed, and distorted how I saw myself and how I presented myself to the world. However, I am in no way trying to avoid responsibility for my actions by referring to my emotional wounds. Everything I did, I chose to do.

I devoted myself to deconstructing my childhood to understand how my wounds influenced my choices (both conscious and unconscious). Like peeling the layers of an onion, I faced each fear one by one, delving within, healing the wounds of my childhood, and changing my conditioning so that I could experience more and more of who I truly was.

This meant connecting with and understanding who I was as a child. Who was Little Tony? The true, authentic essence of who I was, and who I am today. When I was in the darkest time of my life, I was living contrary to my core essence. As I healed I started living more in alignment with Little Tony, and my life started to improve in magnificent ways. Life became less of a struggle and began to flow.

Little Tony remained very much real and alive. We may not see it, relate to it, recognize it, or understand it, but that inner spark is always there. However much we may feel that our spark has been extinguished, it hasn't. No matter who you are and what you've done, no matter how smothered and invisible that spark has become, it still shines. When I experienced this realization the first time, and basked in its inner glow, I cried. For two reasons: first, because I saw the beacon as a way back to my humanity, like a lighthouse; and second, because I realized how disconnected I'd become, not just from the rest of humanity but from myself. That was why for the longest time I wore the mask I call Dark Tony: the mean, hard, and vicious bully who purportedly protected the bullied, the alter ego to Little Tony—the sensitive, shy, bright, intelligent, soft little boy who was hurt so often. Dark Tony and Little Tony were like Dr Jekyll and Mr Hyde with alcohol as the catalyst, the self-medication I used to numb my emotions. I truly believe that the extent to which we dehumanize others is a mirror of how disconnected and dehumanized we are inside.

At a deep core level, I began to understand a phrase that Dōv often repeated: "The quality of my relationship with others is defined by the quality of my relationship with myself." But, like so many personal growth platitudes, it is one thing to know this intellectually and quite another to know it experientially and in your heart. What confirmed the truth of this statement for me was that as I reconnected and rebuilt a relationship with Little Tony, there were immediate changes in my external relationships. People reacted to and treated me differently in ways that were both subtle and not so subtle. How could I expect others to love me when I couldn't love myself? How could I love others fully when I was afraid?

It's as if the way we treat ourselves is written on a sign we wear around our neck that then instructs others how to treat us. If we don't like the way we are being treated, we can change that sign by changing how we treat ourselves and connecting to our inner essence. I believe the closer we can get to our essence, and the more we can let that spark shine through into the world, the happier we will be and the easier life will become.

This often requires us to change negative core beliefs about ourselves, known as toxic shame. There are two types of shame: healthy and toxic. Healthy shame is that transitory feeling when we do something wrong, when we're embarrassed and our cheeks flush; it acts as our moral compass, letting us know when we are operating outside of our personal value system. Toxic shame is not transitory; it is there 24-7, forming part of the subconscious belief system that creates our identity and telling us that we are worthless, not good enough, less than human. Toxic shame is an impaired sense of self that compels us to live our lives in reaction to those false negative beliefs.

We usually pick up negative beliefs about ourselves in childhood. Those are the ones that reside in our subconscious; many are irrational and make no sense at all. Have you ever met a beautiful person who thought they were ugly? A talented person who believed they weren't good enough? Often these beliefs are completely fictional, and here's why:

Before the age of five or six, children's brainwaves are in a hypnagogic, or meditative, state. Ever had someone tell you to be careful what you do or say around children because they soak up information like a sponge? Well, it's true. In that hypnagogic state everything a young child perceives—every word, emotion, or action—goes straight into their subconscious, unfiltered, even if it's a blatant lie or untruth. This is because a young child's rational mind doesn't develop until around age six or seven, yet we use our rational mind to filter information, analyze, and discern what makes sense and what doesn't (which is why, for example, the Catholic Church offers first communion at age seven, when the child is thought to be able to begin to choose). So these perceptions can become the foundation for our belief systems regardless of whether or not they are healthy or even accurate.

All of the belief systems that make up who we think we are and who we project ourselves to be are based on the subjective meaning we give to people, events, and places in our past. The things that were said or not said, the things that were done or not done, all contribute to beliefs and values we hold about ourselves. When we change through healing the subjective meaning we have given people and events in our past, we change our future. If we change a core belief about ourselves, all the self-perceptions based on that core belief also begin to change.

Layer by layer I did this, and with each layer I healed, I became less toxic. I had been denying and hiding my shame for so long that it was spilling out everywhere for everyone to see except me. Toxic shame wasn't just a secret I was keeping from others; it was the dirty little secret I was keeping from myself.

The core beliefs that make up the foundation of our identity affect and filter any new perceptions that arise throughout our lives and actually form part of the rational brain. Like some subconscious and incredibly intricate game of Jenga, these beliefs rely on each other for their integrity, and this is where the ego comes in. The ego's role is to maintain and protect the integrity of that structure. The ego cares not about the accuracy or validity of the underlying beliefs but rather maintaining the structure. To the ego, that Jenga-like structure is everything, and it will stop at nothing, including harmful and even fatal thoughts and actions, to preserve it.

White supremacist ideology became so intertwined with my identity that there was nothing anyone could have said to me to talk me out of my position. There was nothing anyone could have said or done to me to dissuade me from my course of action because it wasn't just what I believed; it was at the heart of who I was, and all of my ego was invested in preserving that.

We can remove, change, and exchange different pieces of the identity structure with ease if they don't threaten or weaken the identity as a whole. Those who are most successful at changing and healing themselves are the ones who remain vigilant and who constantly work on replacing faulty structural pieces with conscious and authentic ones. Over the years, I've witnessed not just my own struggles with ego and identity but also many others' through the group work I've done. I've observed many successes and many failures. I've noticed that when we experience a breakthrough (removing a significant piece of that structure), the ego will insert new pieces in order to stabilize and maintain that structure. These pieces may be the same, or they can be different but distorted enough to maintain the integrity. This is why people often leap forward only to return to their previous state days, weeks, or months later.

The structure is wobbly, which means that process can sometimes look like a person is going backwards, which can fool people into abandoning the change they seek out of fear. "Don't touch that piece," says the ego. "The whole thing will fall down and you will die." The truth is you won't, but your identity might. When I was first in Dōv's office and he asked me to tell him what I was so afraid to say about my past, I experienced a visceral feeling of fear and terror. The reality was that the fear was an illusion that had kept me stuck in the past, until I finally ignored the illusion, faced my fear, and allowed myself to be vulnerable.

I attended a seven-day workshop called "Deep" with a a dozen others, where we delved into healing our deepest childhood wounds. Early in the program we had to reveal something nobody else in the room knew about us. When it was my turn, I knew what I needed to do to make myself utterly vulnerable to the group: I had to reveal my past, which I was still keeping secret from everyone except Dōv.

There it was again: the fear and terror of being rejected by an entire room of people, many of whom were people of colour. As I had done in that literal moment of truth in Dōv's office, I pushed past the fear and for twenty minutes revealed the details of who I had been, as well as the things I had said and done. In my vulnerability I felt naked and afraid. My cheeks were searing red with shame and guilt as I stood in silence afterwards, waiting for the anger, rage, and rejection to come.

But they never did. Theose people looked at me without judgment and with radical compassion, mirroring and teaching me how to love and accept myself in the process, a process that would require time and repetition. Afterwards, realizing that my world hadn't ended (just like in Dōv's office), I felt as if a huge weight had been lifted. Author and researcher Brené Brown captures this feeling beautifully in *The Gifts of Imperfection*: "Because true belonging only happens when we present our authentic, imperfect selves to the world, our sense of belonging can never be greater than our level of self-acceptance."

If we are not who we think we are, then who are we? For me, answering that question required the assistance of someone like Dōv, who could hold up the metaphorical mirror to help me see the real me, not the delusional image of myself that was based on my negative core beliefs. Life itself is a mirror, and it often requires somebody to angle it just right so we can see our true reflection. In doing so, we can, layer by layer, remove the masks we wear and begin to reveal the deeper truth of who we are.

As I gained insight into my destructive journey and the role that toxic shame played in my own life, I started to think about how shame plays out in other people, both as individuals and as groups. Ideology plays a much smaller role than you would think in drawing people to violent extremist groups; rather, I believe toxic shame creates the vulnerabilities in a person that make the ideology seem attractive, as was the case for me. Trauma leaves us with a flawed belief system that forms part of our identity and tells us that we are not lovable enough or smart enough, that we are powerless and weak, that we are less than. And then we go out into the world and live our lives in reaction to that, overcompensating to mask the underlying shame. What is the opposite of shame? Pride. You see it in expressions like "I am just proud of my race" and "white pride," and in the names of far-right groups like the Proud Boys. Sometime we live up to the lie (for example, a gifted underachiever), and sometimes we spend our lives disproving the lie (an overachiever), needing to always be the winner in every transaction (sound familiar?). I chose to embrace an ideology that told me I was greater than to compensate for the feeling of being less than.

Toxic shame takes two forms: one is the shame we develop through our individual experiences and the intergenerational transfer of shame in our families (toxic shame cascades intergenerationally until it is healed); the other is collective shame, when we are made to feel shame for who we are and not for what we've done.

To give you an example of just how insidious toxic collective shame is, consider an academic study that was conducted to look at stereotypes and test results. Two sets of exams were given, and the only difference between them was in the demographic information collected at the top. In one set of exams, students were asked to self-identify by race; the others were not. The students in the first set who identified themselves as black scored significantly less than the black students in the second set—the ones who did not have to answer that question. Simply by thinking of themselves as black before writing the test, those first participants scored lower. As a white supremacist, I used to believe that black people had inferior intelligence and that was why they scored lower. When I learned to look with compassion at the experience of African Americans and the legacy of slavery and white supremacy—in which the concept of being less than human was enshrined in law, systematically keeping them on the bottom rung of society—this kind of outcome made perfect sense. This study is one example of just how deeply buried into the psyche toxic shame can be.

We can see the role of collective shame in the rise of Nazi Germany. The Treaty of Versailles, which ended World War I, left Germany utterly humiliated and the German people filled with shame. Hitler rose to power on the back of a promise to restore German pride and cast off the humiliation of Versailles. Combine this shame with the deaths of 3.4 million men in World War I—deaths that left 3.3 million families fatherless—and is it any wonder that a father figure promising a restoration of national pride and glory to the Fatherland was elected? This is not an excuse for the horrors that followed, but I see it as a tragic example, on a global scale, of how certain vulnerabilities can be manipulated toward evil ends.

James Gilligan was a prison psychiatrist for twenty-five years. In his book *Violence: Reflections on a National Epidemic*, Gilligan says that "all violence is an attempt to replace shame with self-esteem." He continues, "I have yet to see a serious act of violence that was not provoked by the experience of feeling shamed and humiliated, disrespected and ridiculed, and that did not represent the attempt to prevent or undo this 'loss of face'—no matter how severe the punishment, even if it includes death."

In his excellent book *Healing the Shame That Binds You*, counsellor and speaker John Bradshaw explains, "To be shame-bound means that whenever you feel any feeling, need or drive, you immediately feel ashamed. The dynamic core of your human life is grounded in your feelings, needs and drives. When these are bound by shame, you are shamed to the core." Bradshaw writes about how toxic shame is at the root of addictions, eating disorders, perfectionism, rage, arrogance, and pride. These detrimental emotions and behaviours, among many others, mask toxic shame. During the group workshops I did with Dõv, I was able to observe how shame manifested in others. Some expressed it in self-harm and some by being abusive, some through substance abuse and some through their relationship choices. These behaviours are all expressions of a person who is shame-bound, and I would add to them the behaviours enmeshed with violent extremism and overt racism.

Racism itself can be a source of shame. And I was projecting my shame onto the communites I targeted. Hatred rests on a foundation of toxic shame and unresolved anger. Suicide is an extreme expression of internalized shame. According to a 2015 study out of Princeton University called "Mortality and Morbidity in the 21st Century," in the United States, suicide is now the number one cause of death for middle-aged white men, to the extent that white men are the only demographic with a declining life expectancy (however, white men still live an average of five years longer than black men, which is problematic on a number of levels having to do with the long-term effects of ongoing systemic racism against black people in American—a topic too vast to cover here). I believe the shame that drives these suicides is connected to the shame that fuels rising white supremacy. Shame is the alienation of the self and is often accompanied by self-loathing at a deep level, which can then be projected onto others. Shame is self-dehumanization, whereas hate and racism are the external projections of that self-dehumanization. Healing dissolves this foundation of shame and anger, without which the ideology cannot take hold.

If shame is at the core of the problem, how do we heal the shame and therefore the hate?

Compassion. If we accept shame as the flawed belief that we are less than, compassion sees the full magnificence of who we are. When we are compassionate, we reflect someone's whole humanity back at them if they are incapable of seeing it on their own. Imagine if we couldn't ever see our reflection. How would we know if we were beautiful or not? How do we ever know how beautiful we are on the inside?

Compassion is the antidote to shame.

Through compassion, we can build a foundation for understanding and healing for individuals, and for society as a whole. Shame is expressed in a multitude of ways both internally and externally, or, as in my case, both. If shame plays such a large role in the dysfunction of society, what is the cure?

Compassion. Radical compassion.

As humans, we are seemingly in a tug-of-war between our connection and oneness with everything and everyone—the spiritual, or heart-based connection—and our experience of being separate and disconnected from everything and everyone. It is not one or the other; rather, we are always experiencing both at the same time. Whether we like it, accept it, or even believe it, when we harm others, when we harm the collective, we also harm ourselves. When we are a perpetrator and victimize others, as I did, we also hurt ourselves in the process. We dehumanize ourselves as we dehumanize others.

When we choose, instead, to harm ourselves, we place ourselves in both roles—perpetrator and victim—and if we can't reconcile the two, the inner conflict can't help but spill over and damage others. Thus, it's crucial that we heal ourselves for the sake of others.

Compassion for the self is crucial to the healing of the whole. The simple truth is that if we don't heal our pain, we *are* our pain. And when we are our pain, it affects others—and not in a good way.

As within, so without. As above, so below. The macrocosm mirrors the microcosm, and I can look out to the world to uncover buried truths deep within me. Healing the self is a social responsibility, and compassion and healing others is a great way to do that.

One of the hardest lessons I learned during this journey was to feel compassion for myself. This is such an important aspect of the healing process, but for the longest time, I felt I didn't deserve compassion because of the horrific things I had said and done. Radical compassion goes inward as well as outward. I started to understand that the more I have compassion for myself, the more I diminish my capacity to do harm in the world. It's not about whether I feel I deserve compassion, but that the rest of the world deserves to be around a person who is less angry and hurtful.

Just to be clear, there is nothing wrong with anger. Anger is a healthy human emotion, and like all healthy human emotions, it is transitory. Unhealthy emotions stick around until they are resolved; in its unhealthy form, anger becomes rage. There is a well-known saying that goes: "Holding on to anger is like drinking poison and expecting the other person to die." One of the most important lessons Dōv taught me was that unresolved anger always expresses itself as violence, but that most of the time we do that violence to the self. Eating disorders, cutting, substance abuse, playing a sport where you break a bone every other month—these are ways that unresolved anger can manifest as violence to the self. I projected my unresolved anger outward: I listened to music that was angry, I chose a youth subculture that gave me permission to be violent, and I eventually adopted an ideology that provided an intellectual framework to justify that violence.

For true healing and change to take place, both compassion for ourselves and for others must be present. Here's the analogy I like to use: Imagine that in the basement of every house in the neighbourhood there is a drum of toxic radioactive waste that poisons everyone within a one-mile radius. Through compassion I can help my neighbours remove those drums of toxic waste, but if I neglect the drum in my own basement because I don't feel I deserve to remove it, am I not still poisoning my neighbours? That's why we need to clean up our own houses, our own childhood wounds—not for our sake alone but also for those around us. When we cling to our wounds and make an identity out of them, everyone around us suffers.

I learned that I had spent the greater part of fifteen years trying to change the world outside of me in order to soothe my inner wounds, to no avail. Taking to heart Gandhi's words "Be the change you wish to see in the world," I realized I could have far more success changing the world when I changed the world inside of me. By changing who you are in the world, you change the world.

Through the practice of radical compassion, I found my way back to humanity. But I still had a lot more work to do, as I felt obliged to undo some of the harm that I'd done.

CHAPTER 10
FORGIVENESS

IN THAT FIRST COUNSELLING session in his office in 2005, Dōv told me that I had an incredibly important message to share with the world about healing through radical compassion, but with my budding financial career, the thought of speaking publicly about my past still terrified me. I was terrified of how my clients might react, how it would affect my income, and how my friends and acquaintances would respond. I still hid my former white supremacist activities from a lot of people. I was getting better at being vulnerable, but I wasn't totally where I needed to be. *One day!* I kept telling myself. *I'm not ready yet.*

In 2010, I was introduced by phone to former racist skinhead Arno Michaelis, author of *My Life after Hate*. In the 1990s, Arno had been the lead singer of Centurion, a white power band on the Resistance Records label that I used to listen to a lot, so I knew who he was, but we had never met. I read his book eagerly, the similarities between our stories resonating strongly with me. I could relate to the middle-class upbringing, the teenage alcoholism, the descent into the racist skinhead movement, the transformative effect of the birth of his daughter, and the departure from the white supremacist movement into the accepting rave scene. Feeling the need to make a positive impact by speaking out publicly against racism and hatred, Arno started the Life After Hate website, which was dedicated to sharing stories of transformation and to publishing books like his. I was inspired and decided to get involved by joining the board and helping where I could.

In 2011, during Dōv Baron's one-year Authentic Speaking and

Leadership Program, he asked the class of about thirty people to think of their most shameful experience. My brain went straight to the most shameful thing I had done, and a long forgotten—or should I say repressed—memory came to mind as I recalled the night my skinhead crew and I chased a gay man into the darkness of a crawl space in a deserted construction site and then threw stones at him. As that scene played over and over in my mind, I felt that heavy, slow burn of shame in my chest. How could I have forgotten such a thing?

Dõv then said, "I want each of you to go to the front of the class and tell that story."

When it was my turn, I reluctantly took my place at the front of the class and began to recount the story.

"Do it again, but this time feel it," Dõv said.

What do you mean, feel it? I thought. I was feeling a ton of stuff internally, but the external reality didn't match up. From the outside it looked like I narrating that story from afar. My voice was completely disembodied, and I couldn't connect to any of my emotions in front of the class and own what I had done; I was too ashamed.

"Again!" Dõv said. "Tell the story from his perspective."

I tried hard to feel what it must have been like for that man to be alone in the darkness, full of fear. I tried to describe what it must have been like for him.

Dõv then asked me to look at the class and tell him what I saw in their faces.

"Judgment," I replied. They were surprised. Anyone else looking at the class would have seen that they felt compassion for me as I struggled with this exercise. But I could only see judgment.

"Again!" Dõv said, many times.

This went on for almost two hours, until I could connect to my shame. Until I could tell that story as both a perpetrator and as the victim. Until I could fully connect to my emotions and own what I had done.

About two weeks later, I was at a St. Patrick's Day party at a friend's house. Early in the evening, I was introduced to a group of four gay men who were friends of the host. Fresh from my ordeal in front of the group, I felt compelled to share that story with them. I was terrified. Mustering up my courage, I approached the men, asked if I could have a word with them, and pointed to an empty room. They obliged, and as we entered the room, I closed the door behind me.

"There's something I want to share with you," I said. I began to share the story of what I had done, and boy, did I feel it. My face felt like I was standing in front of a furnace.

When I finished, their faces showed a range of emotions from sympathy to anger.

"I know I didn't do it to you, but somebody else did. I did it to someone from your community," I said. "I am so sorry for what I've done. Can you forgive me?"

At this point, tears were rolling down my face, and the faces of three of the men; the fourth remained stoic, his arms crossed in anger. He wasn't in a place where he could forgive, and I had no right to expect that from him. All I could do was present him with an opportunity to forgive, if he so chose. The others hugged me and forgave me, and it seemed that the experience was as cathartic for them as it was for me.

By confessing to members of a community that I had harmed so greatly and receiving compassion and forgiveness in return, I felt like a 1,000-pound gorilla had gotten off my back. I can't know what they felt, but I think the experience may have been about having their pain and mistreatment both acknowledged and apologized for. My guess is that most, if not all, members of the LGBTQ+ community have been attacked, bullied, shamed, humiliated, or discriminated against. They will probably never receive an apology from their tormentor, just as I will most likely never get a chance to apologize directly to the people I have harmed.

When we harm one, we harm the whole. When we can heal the whole, we heal the one. Two of the men I spoke to at the party have since become good friends, and I see them regularly. What transpired that night opened my eyes to how acknowledging the pain and harm that I had caused could create the opportunity for healing in that very community. Sure, it felt nice to be forgiven, and there was certainly a healing aspect to it for me, but the experience was also about giving others the opportunity to heal. My experience planted a seed of intent in me to engage with other communities that I had harmed.

In 2011, Google Ideas (Google's think tank, now called Jigsaw) sponsored the Summit Against Violent Extremism, or SAVE, in Dublin, Ireland. I attended, along with fifty former violent extremists from around the world who were now working for peace and about 150 people working in government, academics, and non-governmental organizations. The former violent extremists present transcended ideology, faith, race, class, and geography. There were former members of the Irish Republican Army and the Ulster Volunteer Force (the pro-British Protestant paramilitary that was the nemesis of the IRA), a former FARC commander from the Revolutionary Armed Forces of Colombia and the former president of Colombia, as well as former Italian Red Brigades, mujahedeen jihadist guerrilla fighters, Al-Shabab East African jihadist fundamentalists, Crips and MS-13 gang members, neo-Nazis, skinheads, and other terrorist and extremist groups.

Also present were survivors of terrorist violence. Included were Jo Berry, a British peace activist whose father was killed by the IRA in the Brighton hotel bombing targeting Margaret Thatcher and the Conservative Party in 1984, who now tours and lectures with the former IRA member who planted the bomb; Gill Hicks, who lost her leg in the 7/7 bombings by radical Islamic terrorists in London in 2005; Amanda Lindhout (author of *A House in the Sky*), a Canadian journalist who was kidnapped in 2008 and held hostage for fifteen months by Islamist insurgents in Somalia; as well as many others who suffered at the hands of violent extremists.

For me, the most interesting part of the three-day conference was not the panel discussions but the side conversations I had with former extremists around meals and at the bar. I was struck by how many similarities there were between the stories of those who joined and then left violent extremist groups. Personal reasons for joining an extremist group were repeated over and over: a search for belonging, significance, brotherhood, community, and purpose, as if the ideologies themselves were secondary. Whether the people I spoke with were right wing, left wing, religious, or from a street gang, these familiar themes seemed woven into almost everyone's story.

When people discussed their reasons for leaving, two themes stood out. One was the birth of a child. The other was receiving compassion from someone they felt they didn't deserve it from—the very definition of radical compassion. Arno Michaelis tells a story of being overwhelmed by the unconditional warmth he encountered when he was ordering a burger at McDonald's and the elderly African American cashier saw the swastika tattooed on his hand and said: "You're a better person than that. I know that's not who you are." Frank Meeink, former white supremacist skinhead gang member and inspiration for the film *American History X*, describes the compassion and consideration shown him by a Jewish antique dealer who hired him despite the big swastika tattoo on his neck.

The summit brought together the co-founders of what would become the non-profit organization Life After Hate: Frank Meeink, author of *Autobiography of a Recovering Skinhead*; Arno Michaelis; Christian Picciolini, Sammy Rangel, a former Latino gang leader who was considered Wisconsin's most violent inmate before he became a social worker; Angela King, a former neo-Nazi skinhead who went to prison for her role in the armed robbery of a Jewish-owned video store and then, after her release, completed three back-to-back degrees; T.J. Leyden, a former skinhead who was one of the first to start helping people leave the movement; Tim Zaal, a former skinhead who now volunteers at the Museum of Tolerance in Los Angeles; and me. Truly inspired by what we had learned and experienced at the conference, we all vowed to continue working together once we got home to North America. We set out with the desire to help people who were where we once were: specifically, to help people leave hate groups, particularly white supremacy groups. There's a picture taken of us on a rooftop courtyard with all our hands piled on top of each other's as we stood in a circle, arms stretched into the middle. All for one, and one for all! On that rooftop, Life After Hate was born.

Now I had a real sense of meaning and purpose. I had a vehicle through which I could turn my dark journey into something positive and begin to heal the harm I had done, which wouldn't have been possible without the self-healing first. I was on my way to realizing the vision of me and my message that Dõv had been able to see when I couldn't.

By August 2011, Life After Hate had filed for 501(c)(3) non-profit status. All the co-founders of Life After Hate came from a white supremacist background except for Sammy Rangel, who'd been involved in a Latino street gang in Chicago. Sammy served many years in prison before becoming a social worker in a remarkable tale of transformation, which he tells in his book *Fourbears: Myths of Forgiveness*, and his TED Talk, "The Power of Forgiveness." When we left the movement, no organizations existed to help those who decided to leave hate and violence behind. Each of us had stumbled through the wilderness and made it back to humanity on our own. Yes, we had mentors and other help, but there were no programs to specifically support people looking to get out. What if we could share our stories and our understanding of that difficult journey to help others who were where we once were? The mission of Life After Hate thus officially became: To inspire individuals to a place of compassion and forgiveness, for themselves and for all people. This also became my personal mission statement. I knew I still had a lot of work to do to atone for my past.

On August 5, 2012, forty-year-old Wade Michael Page fatally shot six people and wounded four others at the Sikh temple in Oak Creek, Wisconsin, before killing himself. One of the six massacred that day was Satwant Singh Kaleka, the temple president. This devastating event recalled the brutal murder of Sikh temple caretaker Nirmal Singh Gill fourteen years earlier in Surrey, British Columbia. Both Gill and Kaleka were sixty-five at the time of their murders and very involved with their respective temples. Both men left the Punjab in the 1980s to start a new life away from the ethnic strife brewing in northern India at the time. Both men displayed exceptional bravery in defence of their temple and community, as Gill fought to keep his sacred *kara* bracelet and as Kaleka attempted to defend his congregants against a man armed with a semi-automatic pistol with only a butter knife before being gunned down. Michael Wade Page was associated with the Hammerskins, which had a thriving chapter in Surrey when Nirmal was slain. Although the two murders might appear random or disconnected, these two men died at the hands of the same loosely connected network of white supremacy.

Not long after, *Georgia Straight* contributor Gurpreet Singh invited me onto his Radio India show in Surrey. In my conversation with Gurpreet, I conceded that all of the fear and hatred I put out into the community contributed to the toxic environment in which Gill's 1998 murder took place. White supremacist ideology, when left unchecked, always ends in murder, and Gill's death is yet another tragic reminder. What was the result of his death? Fear. An entire community living in mortal fear. Balwant Singh Gill, the president of the Surrey temple at the time, explained the feeling of fear by saying, "If it can happen to Nirmal, it can happen to anyone."

The skinheads who committed that murder were known to me, recruited by people I had helped recruit. They partied with the same people, and at the same places, I had not long before. Words do matter, and the energy we put out into the world has a long-lasting effect even after we are gone. It's just like throwing a pebble in the pond. We never get to see the ripple land on the opposite shore. Everything we say, everything we do, who we choose to be will have an effect and consequence, either positive or negative. Love or fear. The ripples from my past are still out there, and I feel compelled to take actions against them. When two big waves travel toward each other and meet, they cancel each other out.

On Singh's show, I took questions and comments from callers from the local Indo-Canadian community. I was taken aback by how positive they were. I had expected at least some callers to be very angry with me, but they weren't. I acknowledged their pain and apologized, owned the harm I had done to their community, and felt the cathartic release.

I was greatly encouraged by this and am now connected to the Punjabi community in Vancouver, a community I once harmed. I have had the opportunity to spend time at the gurdwaras in both Surrey and Wisconsin. To spend a day with Nirmal's son-in-law and one of Satwant's two sons, Amardeep. To see the place where Nirmal died and to meditate in the large hall at the gurdwara in Oak Creek where the congregants were gunned down. To see the bullet hole in the steel door frame to the main hall and realize how large a cavity a 9mm pistol round makes. To listen to the families' pain and loss, and offer my sorrow and regret at participating in and growing the movement that birthed these actions. When we do and say things (good or evil), we rarely get to witness the immediate impact, the end result. The gurdwaras in Surrey and Wisconsin are reminders of the impact of fear and the end product of hate. We must learn from them.

We know where fear takes us, but what about love and connection? At the Oak Creek Temple, I was blown away by the renovations undertaken so that the place of worship now has seven domes to symbolize each person who died that day. Who was the seventh, you ask? Wade Michael Page. Even in their anger and grief, the Sikh community survivors recognized the humanity in someone who had dehumanized their community so grotesquely and caused so much pain. I was awestruck and thoroughly inspired by their level of spiritual awareness in the face of such tragedy, as much as I was moved by the long hug I received from Nirmal's son-in-law after our day together. We can learn much from these men and their communities.

Galvanized by these healing interactions, I wanted to apologize properly to different family members who had been affected by my white supremacist activities. I asked Dōv for guidance on how to best do that. The process he recommended was simple in concept but a little more difficult in practice. It starts with a simple question: "How did what I did affect you?" The next step is to shut up and listen. No excuses, no deflections, no responses—just listen, without interrupting the other person. Take in how what you did made them feel. Then you can truly say you're sorry and apologize. The word "sorry" is often thrown around too easily, without any emotional connection. But if we ask that question and then truly listen to the person's response, we can get to a place of true remorse for the pain we have caused. I heard for the first time the shame my mother endured as a flight attendant handing out newspapers with my picture on the front page. I have caused all of my family members an incredible amount of pain with the shame I brought upon the family.

After seeing the positive effects in people who had generously forgiven me, I also took the opportunity to forgive others. As I continued along this path of compassion and understanding, I began to look at my relationship with Michelle, the mother of my two children, who had left the country, leaving me a single father. For the longest time, I was so angry not just at Michelle but at women in general, and I had major trust issues in that regard. Incapable of taking any responsibility for myself, I had laid the blame for my troubles at the feet of all women and held extremely negative attitudes toward them, with the exception of my mother and my daughter. Since I didn't have a healthy view of women to begin with, my attitudes at my lowest ponit were downright toxic. I regularly used my children as human shields against relationships and intimacy. My anger remained reserved for those outside our little family unit, yet slowly but surely—and very cautiously—the transformation of my heart continued. I continued to learn about relationships, relationship patterns, and how to have a healthy relationship, as well as how to love myself. Eventually, I met my fiancée, Rhiannon, and we have a healthy, loving relationship based on respect and equality.

As for Michelle, after the end of our relationship, my view of her was as a woman who had left me with two small children and a whole lot of resentment. But what was the story behind her pain? Michelle's mother had abandoned her at the same age Michelle was when she left me with the two children. It wasn't her fault. Once I viewed Michelle and her history through the lens of compassion, I could understand that she did the best she could with what she knew at the time. Instead of continuing to be angry with her, I came to realize that she had given the children and me one of the greatest gifts that she could in leaving (though it was not obvious back then). She returned to Canada with a new family when our kids were in their teens, and they were able to reconnect. Through my compassion for myself, I was able to have compassion for her, and I came to a place where forgiveness was possible. Forgiveness is about you and not the other person, so you can forgive someone without them knowing. I did just that with Michelle, releasing myself from the anger and resentment I had carried for so long. I felt liberated.

Forgiving my father was the next. Forgiveness doesn't mean letting the other person off the hook, and it doesn't mean forgetting what happened. Forgiveness is about letting go of the long-held anger and resentment. In looking at my father's history through the lens of compassion, I couldn't help but wonder about his childhood. I had a father who was there physically but was emotionally unavailable. His father was away at sea most of the time, either in the merchant navy during World War II or as a chief steward on a luxury liner crossing the Atlantic. Thus, my father's relationship with his father was with a provider who was never really there. The difference with my father was that he slept, ate, and drank in the same house as the rest of us but was emotionally distant. It was easy to see how a pure, loving little child could learn emotional numbness from war, bombs, and abandonment. I could see how the pursuit of intellectual superiority above all else could become honed as an integral survival skill. I couldn't help but wonder who he would have been without the dark clouds of his past. As I asked that question, I was compelled to ask it of myself as well: *Who would I have been without the dark clouds of abandonment, the beatings, the ridicule, and the anger?*

Emotional trauma can exist without physical abuse through experiences like abandonment and neglect, and for me, the emotional pain was worse than the physical pain of the beatings. In her manifesto "Every Smack Is a Humiliation," Swiss psychologist Alice Miller writes, "In the short term, corporal punishment may produce obedience. But it is a fact documented by research that in the long term the results are inability to learn, violence and rage, bullying, cruelty, inability to feel another's pain, especially that of one's own children, even drug addiction and suicide, unless there are enlightened or at least helping witnesses on hand to prevent that development."

As a child I needed to feel loved and be told that I was loved, that I mattered, that I was significant, wanted, and appreciated. I wanted my accomplishments noticed and approved of. My father worked sixty hours a week and usually came home after I was in bed. Sometimes I would get ten or twenty minutes with him during the kiss goodnight. I thought my dad was the best and I put him on a pedestal. I know that in his own way he loved us very much, but his way of demonstrating that was to provide our family with all our needs. "Work is love made visible" is a memorable Kahlil Gibran quote that perfectly describes my father's approach.

If our partners or loved ones express their commitment to us in ways we don't understand, the result can be a great deal of hurt. A boy of four, five, or six doesn't understand the meaning of hard work, or what it costs to run a household. What he does understand is that his father is too busy, tired, drunk, or simply not there to spend time with him.

My father grew up in the Catholic slums of Liverpool, near the docks in a small tenement with five brothers. At the age of four or five, as the bombing campaign of Liverpool got underway during World War II, he was sent away for a time to stay with his aunt Annie, who lived away from the town centre. His brothers were allowed to stay home. The perceived rejection by his mother—sending him into the arms of another woman—is a wound that overshadowed his entire life. It set up a pattern of triangulation that was at the core of his relationship with his mistress and, in fact, at the core of most of his relationships.

Later, while his father was lost at sea and presumed dead after his ship was torpedoed, my father's older brother Joe took on the role of man of the house, and my dad was very jealous of the close relationship Joe had with their mother, a relationship it seemed like he could never have.

This meant that the moment I was conceived, my mom changed, in the eyes of my father, from a hot stewardess wife into my mother. This forever altered the dynamic of their relationship, and it also changed the dynamic of my relationship with them. From that point on, my father projected all of his mother issues onto her, and his jealousy issues with his brother onto me. It's easy to see how, in a new country, with no social network, my mother turned me into her primary emotional relationship. My father has always been insanely jealous of my relationship with my mother, and it was a source of derision. Growing up, it was palpable. I remember being around seven or eight and sitting on the couch reading with my mom when my dad walked in and said, "Oh, don't you two make a lovely looking couple." What chance did I ever have to bond with my father if I was my mother's primary emotional relationship? This was a deep source of rage that I only uncovered much later in life.

"So what?" you may ask. Lots of people had worse childhoods and didn't end up as white supremacists. Boo-hoo, just because you've got some mommy-daddy issues doesn't give you licence to be an asshole.

And you would be right. I clearly wasn't the only kid who grew up with adultery in the home or was beaten at Catholic school. These aspects of my past aren't excuses but rather the foundation for understanding and healing. Sometimes I wonder which is worse: to be abandoned by someone thousands of miles away, or to feel the abandonment of someone living and breathing in the same house as you? My father's pain became my pain, but I realized he was just parenting the way he was taught.

And here is where a big lesson in compassion and forgiveness kicked in. Just as I was moved by the birth of my children—which showed me how we all come into this world with wonder and boundless, unconditional love—my deeper understanding of my experiences with my father revealed that we don't start out as assholes. Rather, this behaviour is something we are taught, something we learn through our experiences. In my case, I embraced and excelled at being an asshole.

This is where the radical compassion part comes. It's easy to feel compassion for people we like or people for whom we feel pity or sorrow, but try having compassion for someone in your life who is the source of your anger. I can sit here and list all the reasons why

I can and should be angry with my father (and thereby the world in general), but where does that get me other than angry? If I'm constantly living my life in anger and in reaction to him, do I not also put him somewhat in control of my emotional state? That is what I did for most of my life.

When I started to look at my father's childhood in an effort to understand him, through the lens of empathy and compassion, it was hard to remain angry. How could I be angry at the four- or five-year-old child who went through such pain? The more I had compassion for my father, the more I healed myself in the process. I felt so deeply and personally wounded by his actions or inactions, as if he chose to treat me the way he did because there was something deficient in me. But I realized it wasn't my fault. There was nothing flawed about me that invited his behaviour; he was simply reliving his childhood wounds, and we were all cast in a specific role in this great family drama. I understood and accepted his limitations and set my boundaries around that. It is said that all suffering comes from either getting what you don't want or not getting what you do want. So much of the pain in our lives comes from expecting something from a person who is incapable of giving it. In the process of forgiveness we aren't justifying or making excuses for what was done, and like with compassion, we have to set healthy boundaries and consequences. But there is no point in me carrying anger at my father for not giving me something he was incapable of. How does that serve me? Part of my spiritual practice is learning to accept things as they are, not how I want them to be. When we accept things as they are and act accordingly, we experience much less pain. I went from believing he didn't love me because I am unlovable to understanding he didn't show he loved me because he didn't know how. It wasn't my fault. The sad part was that he was a psychiatrist, but he never did the deep work on himself. Remember the one about the cobbler's kids who go shoeless? Exactly.

Another big revelation was that for most of my adult life there was a very clear pattern to my relationships with men. One of my fondest memories was of riding in my dad's little sports car, driving up and down a stretch of highway as I fantasized that he was Batman and I was Robin. That experience set me up to find a Batman to whom I could be Robin in an idealized relationship resembling the one I had with my father as a child. From the biker I lived with as a young man to Wolfgang Droege, Tom Metzger, and Ernst Zündel, and even Dōv, there has been a whole host of older men with whom I slid into the Robin role in search of the approval I so needed and craved from my father. The grander my activities in the white supremacist movement, the more pats on the back, praise, and approval I received. For a time, I was happy revelling in this new-found attention and glory.

It wasn't until much later, when I found myself in a business relationship with the dynamics reversed, that I was able to fully see the true nature of such relationships and how disempowering they are. On the surface, Batman and Robin are known as the dynamic duo, which sounds pretty cool. On closer inspection, however, it becomes obvious that the relationship is inherently unequal. Batman has all the power and Robin has none. The Batman-Robin dynamic is missing an essential ingredient of a healthy relationship: equality. I was willing to give up all of my power, over and over, for a few crumbs of acknowledgment and approval. That need for approval was a big one, and no matter how hard I tried, I could never unlock that puzzle with my father. I found it easily, though, among the father figures to whom I gravitated. Once I had that replacement, the relationship with my father was one of anger and contempt. At times I became so hurtful toward him that it seemed our relationship would never recover. It was a love-hate relationship that kept me in my father's orbit: I was constantly trying to attain his love, but once I found that elsewhere, all that was left was the hate. There was a point when there was no coming back to try to win his approval. But in getting to that place of understanding through compassion, I found peace with him. I also offered him a heartfelt apology and asked him a question: "How did what I did affect you?" Then I listened without judgment or interruption as he recalled the personal and professional shame he experienced, as well as all the pain I had caused him. The relationship with my father is no longer charged with anger, resentment, or triggers.

One of the most difficult questions for me was: Do I forgive the teacher who beat me in grade six? I struggled with that one until the universe decided it was time. While I was in Brazil for the World Cup in 2014, one of the families travelling in our group had a son who went to Vancouver College. He had just finished grade six, and I asked him who his teacher was. I was stunned to hear it was the same teacher who had beaten me thirty years earlier. Immediately, a rush of emotions flooded over me. Over the next few weeks after returning home, I ran into two other people from my Vancouver College days who had been taught by the same teacher. The coincidence was too much, and I knew it was a sign that I needed to reconcile my lingering anger and resentment.

I wrote the teacher an email summarizing my life's journey and the part he had played. Given his religious affiliations, the letter was framed this way:

> God has interesting ways to illuminate the way for us. I was at the World Cup in Rio with a group that included a student of yours, and your name came up and with it a lot of resentment at some of the things I experienced in grade 6. I came home and forgot about it but thought to myself I should contact

you to release and heal whatever resentment there may be. I was recently reminded and inspired about forgiveness when the man who shot the Pope was released from prison and went to visit his tomb. I have always been inspired by the Pope's visit to that man in prison. In the last 2 months I have met three people that went to VC in and around the time that I was there and 2 of them were taught by you, I believe. We joked about oldie moldies! I believe there is a piece of compassion and forgiveness that I have overlooked or avoided, and as part of my own healing process I have decided that now is the time to reach out to you to help me so that I can let go of some lingering resentments. I believe people do the best they can with what they know at the time, and that is what I think Jesus meant when he said from the cross, "Father, forgive them, for they know not what they do." The most powerful way I can do this is if we could meet in person over a coffee or something. I understand if you are not comfortable with this. I want you know that I am not angry or blaming anything on you, but I would like the opportunity to forgive you in person.

I wasn't surprised that I didn't get a response. But I didn't need a response because forgiveness isn't about the other person—the other person doesn't even have to know. Forgiving Brother Gianti was a gift I could give myself, and now he no longer has the power to hijack my emotional state. Forgiveness gives us freedom from the shackles of our past. Dr Fred Luskin, author of *Forgive for Good* and director and co-founder of the Stanford Forgiveness Project, says, "When we choose forgiveness, we release our past to heal our present." Dr Luskin's Forgiveness Project and Stanford have done some stunning research into the psychological and physiological benefits of forgiveness. The research shows that anger and hostility are detrimental to our cardiovascular systems, contributing to heart attack, high blood pressure, and stroke. Psychologically speaking, research subjects showed less stress, anger, depression, and anxiety, as well as increased self-confidence. Don't just take the forgiveness thing from me, listen to the science: "The most powerful way to heal is through forgiveness," Luskin writes. "When we forgive, we take something less personally, blame the person who hurt us less and change our grievance story. Through learning the process of forgiveness, we can forgive anyone who has hurt us in any way."

As I grew to understand the transformative benefit of forgiving others and releasing past angers and resentments, I embarked on a journey to give other people—people from communities I had harmed—an opportunity to release their own anger and resentment over my actions or the actions of others who espoused the same white supremacist ideology, racism, and anti-Semitism as I had.

CHAPTER 11
TSHUVAH: ATONEMENT

DURING MY VERY FIRST counselling session with Dōv in 2005, I discovered I still had some internal unresolved residue regarding, in particular, my role in Holocaust denial. When I was active in the white supremacist movement, I had concluded, based on cherry-picked data and information that I had used to form erroneous conclusions, that the data and the historical record didn't reconcile, thus calling into question the truth about the Holocaust.

I remember going to a Holocaust Remembrance Day education session at the University of British Columbia in high school at the age of seventeen and having nothing but contempt and derision for the survivors and their day of "brainwashing." With my ego and intellect hand in hand, I listened to every word, every story, like a lion on the savannah waiting for its prey, for the slightest inconsistency or contradiction to prove and validate my belief at the time that the history of the Holocaust was steeped in lies. The moment such a thing appeared, my ego would pounce and declare to the world through me: "Half the numbers don't add up!" "The date is wrong!" "How come on the plaque at Auschwitz they changed the number from 4 million to 1.5 million?" In my ignorance and disconnection I couldn't see the error in my approach: one was too many. In one fell swoop, I would throw the baby out with the bathwater and declare that all of the facts must be suspect. You see, my ego was okay denying the suffering of so many if it could find some inconsistency to justify it. Such is the nature of the ego, especially when it is divorced from the heart like mine was.

I had known Ernst Zündel quite well, and I had become well versed in the dogma of Holocaust denial. I had met David Irving a couple of times and built an interactive online guide to Auschwitz for John Ball. I knew all of the questions and arguments that contradicted the historical record of the Holocaust.

In the world of Holocaust denial, nobody says that nothing happened at Auschwitz. They will acknowledge cruelty, executions, typhoid epidemics, and a whole host of reasons to try to explain that the people who died were not exterminated. And some of the arguments can be very compelling. Therein lies the rub: it is possible to make convincing arguments about just about anything if one is willing to ignore contradictory evidence and focus solely on the facts that supposedly support the chosen theory. I didn't take the Holocaust at face value, nor did I look at all of the factual information to make the correct analysis. Again, the ego is always searching for evidence of what it believes to be true. Driven by my ego's need to be right, combined with the underlying white supremacist ideological agenda against Jews, I cherry-picked to build my case. Back then, I saw the Holocaust not as historical fact but rather a grand deception or hoax that was perpetrated to garner worldwide sympathy for Jews, a sympathy that enhanced what I saw as their malignant power to control the world. To destroy that sympathy was to destroy that power. And twenty years later, I had never circled back to look at those old beliefs. To be clear, after my inward journey, I no longer challenged the historical record of what happened in the Holocaust, but I had lingering unresolved contradictions in the back of my mind that I had avoided examining. Anti-Semitism is sometimes the most difficult bias to resolve because of the deep complexities of the popular conspiracy theories. They take time to learn and more time to unlearn.

Fast-forward to Orlando, Florida, in December 2013. Angela

King, my colleague at Life After Hate, was speaking at the Holocaust Memorial Resource and Education Center in advance of a much larger event in Fort Lauderdale, where she would be delivering a keynote to all of the tenth-grade students in Broward County as part of the state-mandated Holocaust education program. After her evening talk, we were given the opportunity to visit the small museum next door. The museum was a single room with glass cases on the wall containing black-and-white photos with information cards, yellowed by age. This was the first time I had visited anything related to the Holocaust since I'd begun my journey to heal. The work I had done had put an end to my dehumanizing others, but I hadn't revisited the Holocaust. The racism faded away quite quickly, as did the hatred I had felt for Jews, but I hadn't returned to this particular subject. Part of me was afraid to admit I was wrong to have held those beliefs, and another part of me was afraid of being right. There was so much damage to undo, and I had focused almost solely on my own healing to this point.

I walked slowly through the museum, taking in every photo and reading every card with an open heart. And with each display, I felt my heart getting heavier and heavier. My chest grew tight, and I started to get a queasy and sinking feeling in my stomach. These sensations may be familiar and common to some, but mine had been suppressed since childhood. This was the first time in my life I was feeling them in the context of the Holocaust.

When I went to bed at the hotel that night, I couldn't sleep. The heaviness was shifting, and my chest and cheeks began to burn with shame. Reflecting on the images and scenes of ordinary people being subjected to extraordinary suffering for no reason other than who they were born to be, understanding that there had been an incalculable amount of suffering and murder, made sleep impossible. And then, at 4:30 a.m., like lightning: it hit me.

How could I feel anyone else's pain when I couldn't and wouldn't look at and feel my own pain? My denial of the suffering of Jews during the Holocaust was an external reflection of my personal denial of my own pain. I couldn't feel for others what I couldn't see in myself. Only through facing and accepting and feeling my own emotional pain was I able to feel, relate to, and acknowledge the pain of others. Just as I had been more than willing to share my pain and suffering by projecting it onto others, I was willing to project the denial of my pain and suffering onto others. No example illustrates this better than the unyielding Holocaust denial I had professed. It is of course incredibly important to recognize that there is no comparison between the pain suffered by the people whose fate I had read about hours earlier and my own pain. But I had to acknowledge that the numbness I was feeling prohibited the recognition of either. This brings me back to my intention, and the mission statement of Life After Hate: To inspire individuals to a place of compassion and forgiveness, for themselves and for all people.

Even though intellectually I understood the notion that self-compassion is necessary in order to feel compassion for others, the visit to the museum hit it home like a sledgehammer. I had always felt guilt or lack of deserving about self-compassion. *Oh, good for you! How nice you can forgive yourself!* But self-compassion and self-forgiveness are essential if one is to offer the same to others in a truly authentic way. Just as forgiveness is not about the other person, self-forgiveness is not about me. I could not see the pain of others until I could see my own. I could not feel their pain until I could feel my own. The more my capacity for self-compassion and forgiveness, the greater my capacity for compassion and forgiveness for others. The most selfish thing I could do was to ignore my own pain, because in doing so, I couldn't help but ignore the suffering of others. At most, I would be left with a mere intellectual acknowledgment of circumstance, not the true feelings of empathy and compassion that drive the desire to alleviate that suffering in others. This is the essence of radical compassion.

Exhausted, I closed my eyes and fell into a deep sleep until my alarm woke me up at five a.m. After hitting the Snooze button, I headed for the shower to get ready for the three-hour drive to Fort Lauderdale. On thirty minutes of sleep and not knowing what the day had in store, I thought, *This is going to be a long day.*

Angela and I arrived at the convention centre and settled in with about 800 students who were seated in tables of ten, with a Holocaust survivor at each table. As we were walking around the room, trying to decide which table to sit at, Angela grabbed me and told me she wanted to introduce me to someone. We walked up to a very sprightly elderly woman I would come to know as Rita Hofrichter. She was a dynamo and a real bundle of energy as she enthusiastically shook my hand and ushered me to join her table. I listened intently as different speakers took the stage. This was my first opportunity to hear Angela tell her compelling story of being bullied and becoming a skinhead, taking part in the armed robbery of a Jewish-owned business and going to prison, and falling in love with a black woman. Then it was Rita's turn to share the harrowing tale of joining the resistance as a young woman and escaping the Warsaw Ghetto after she obtained false papers. Their stories couldn't have been more different, but both were very emotional, and the students listened with rapt attention.

It was then time for the participants at the tables to do some exercises. The Holocaust survivor at each table spent about twenty minutes telling their story in detail. Rita did the same, delving into greater detail than she had in her earlier speech. She had smuggled herself out of the Warsaw Ghetto with false papers after participating in the Ghetto Uprising and survived by hiding in a Catholic convent orphanage. Listening to her story, I began to feel that familiar feeling of shame. It is one thing to read about events in a textbook or see them depicted on the big screen and dismiss them; it is something else altogether to look a human being in the eye while they are authentically recalling their story and deny that.

The students were asked to share their thoughts after hearing the keynotes and the survivor's story at their table. As I listened to the students one by one, I felt compelled to share my history as a former neo-Nazi who had denied the Holocaust. Looking Rita directly in the eyes, I expressed my regret and shame at my actions while sharing my journey (including my experience from the night before) so that the students at the table could hear my story and learn from it. My eyes welled with tears as, in that moment, I felt utterly naked in my vulnerability.

What happened next blew me away. Rita reached across the table, grabbed me by the hand, looked me in the eye, and said, "I forgive you."

Just as with the gay men at the party, and with the Indo-Canadian callers to Gurpreet Singh's radio show, I can't overstate how powerful it is to feel radical compassion and forgiveness from someone I didn't feel I deserved it from. It is powerful for both parties. Rita had already learned the transformative nature of the gift she was both giving and receiving, as she was aware that her compassion and forgiveness had had a powerful impact on Angela years before. The exchange has the potential to lift the heart and soul of both people involved, and I was left feeling cleansed. In this way, I was able to let Rita's compassion and forgiveness wash over me. Rita Hofrichter passed away in 2016, at the age of eighty-nine.

Learning how to receive such a gift had been one of my greatest challenges on my journey, but there were still deeper lessons for me to discover about apologies, atonement, and forgiveness.

In 2017, I was meeting with Alan, one of my financial clients, who is Jewish. We were discussing the work that I was doing for Life After Hate. I asked Alan about his own experiences with racism and anti-Semitism and how they affected him. He described how his mother kept a packed suitcase with a passport and some money in the closet by the front door in case the authorities came for the Jews again, like the Nazis did during the Holocaust. I acknowledged to him that this was a fear I had helped perpetuate and keep very much alive. I told Alan that I had spoken to Jewish communities around the world but never to the community in Vancouver, the Jewish community that I had harmed the most. You see, it was easy for me to share my story with Jewish communities outside of Vancouver because it wasn't as personal, because I hadn't harmed them directly. The Vancouver Jewish community was conspicuous by its absence. I told Alan I was unsure if I could even approach the community. "I can help you with that!" he said excitedly, and then, like all good Jews do when they meet a former neo-Nazi, he called his rabbi.

Rabbi Dan Moskovitz, or Rabbi Dan, as everyone calls him, is the rabbi for the reform congregation at Temple Sholom in Vancouver. I went to see Rabbi Dan in the spring and told him that I wanted to do something to make amends to the Jewish community in Vancouver. We had a long conversation in his office in which I shared my history and my journey as he gauged my sincerity and authenticity. At the end of the meeting, he said he knew just the week for me to come before his congregation, and he picked a Saturday in September for my visit. The Saturday he chose was the week before Rosh Hashanah, which is the Jewish New Year and begins the ten days of repentance that lead up to Yom Kippur, the Day of Atonement, the holiest day of the year in Judaism, when Jews ask for forgiveness for their transgressions. The service on that Saturday is called Selichot, which means "forgiveness." The event was to be called "*Tshuvah* of a White Supremacist."

In the Jewish tradition, *tshuvah* means "return" and describes the return to God and our fellow human beings that is made possible through repentance for our wrongs. One of the best definitions of sin I ever heard described it as any thought or action that separates us from ourselves, our families, our society, or our creator, which means that every thought or action has the consequence of creating either connection or disconnection. Transgressions before God require confession, sincere remorse, and doing everything in one's power to undo the damage done, but when it comes to damage done to another person, the process gets a little more complicated. Restitution is a requirement, and we must ask forgiveness. The wronged party is under no obligation to forgive, but not forgiving after three requests is in itself a sin. This process is further complicated because in the case of slander or libel—spreading false Jewish tropes and conspiracies with the aim of spreading suspicion and hate, for example—how does one possibly ask for forgiveness from everyone they harmed? Impossible.

When the day of the event in September rolled around, I was nervous, apprehensive, and unsure what to expect. Onstage I shared my history, the misdeeds that I had committed against the local Jewish community, and the work that I do now to try to repair the harm. This was an incredibly powerful evening for me because I shared with the congregation that my very first act of anti-Semitism was to put a National Front sticker on the front door of that very same synagogue thirty years before. Everything was now coming full circle back to Temple Sholom. Pausing to let that statement sink in, I could hear the gasps from the audience as the realization dawned that this synagogue was indeed ground zero for my descent into anti-Semitism.

Afterwards, I spoke to many of the congregants one on one, and I was surprised by how many shook my hand and thanked me. Like when I spoke with members of the Indo-Canadian community on Gurpreet Singh's radio show, my expectation was that at least someone would yell at me, but perhaps that expectation is a projection of my own feelings of unworthiness. That evening, I was hugged, thanked, and forgiven by so many people, people who belonged to a community that I had once harmed. I felt healed by their compassion and forgiveness, but I also saw a weight lifted from those who had their pain acknowledged and apologized for.

Not long after my experience at Temple Sholom, another opportunity arose to further my journey of healing for myself and for others. There was a chance for me to be best man at a close friend's wedding in Budapest, Hungary, two weeks before Rhiannon and I were planning to attend the 2018 World Cup in Kaliningrad, Russia. Looking at the map as we planned our trip, I moved my finger in a straight line from Budapest to Kaliningrad to see what was in between. The path went right through Auschwitz. Without hesitation, I decided it was time to make this vital visit.

In Budapest, Rhiannon and I stayed at an Airbnb close to where all the wedding festivities would be taking place. While walking around and exploring the neighbourhood, we came across a memorial to the Jews who had been forced to move into the Budapest Ghetto, which consisted of several blocks of the old Jewish quarter. Looking through peepholes in the wall, we could see magnified images of the vibrant Jewish community that used to occupy the same streets we walked on and live in the same buildings that stood all around us. The buildings are still there, but the flourishing Jewish community is virtually gone (recently, there has been a small revival of the Jewish community in that quarter). On closer inspection of the mural that depicted the boundaries of the ghetto, one thing immediately stood out. Our Airbnb was, in fact, a building inside the walls of the Budapest Ghetto. We were staying in an apartment that had once been occupied by Jews, and then emptied during that dark time.

Two days later, we visited the Shoes on the Danube Bank, a memorial that is both literal and metaphorical. In front of the Parliament buildings, on the bank of the Danube River, is a row of about sixty pairs of iron shoes in a permanent sculpture to remind people of the executions of as many as 20,000 Jews from the ghetto in the winter of 1944–45. They were killed by the fascist Arrow Cross militia, who ordered them to take off their shoes and then shot them at the water's edge so that their bodies were carried away. The empty shoes are a stark reminder of a community that was destroyed. Between May and July of 1944, more than 400,000 Hungarian Jews were deported to Auschwitz. Less than one-third of Hungary's prewar Jewish population of 825,000 survived the Holocaust. If what I was feeling in Budapest was so dark and heavy, what was in store for me at Auschwitz?

Peter Hutchison, director and producer of *Healing from Hate: Battle for the Soul of a Nation*, an examination of the root causes of hate group activity, volunteered to document my journey to Auschwitz so that others could learn from it. But I would have made this journey whether it was filmed or not. The purpose of the trip was twofold. First, in addition to healing myself, I hoped that my encounters with people along the way would provide an opportunity for them to experience some healing. And by recording the process, the trip could be used to inspire many more to begin a healing process of their own and with the people around them. Second, I intended to bear witness to the atrocities that were perpetrated and document that journey to serve as an educational piece for young people and other who are where I once was: a neo-Nazi, white supremacist, and Holocaust denier. I believe the lessons I have learned about myself along the way are universal, and if I can transform my darkness into light, I hope I can inspire others to do the same. Given the current world political climate of increasingly vocal and visible hate groups and hateful rhetoric, I think it's imperative to remind ourselves, with a fresh perspective, what human beings are capable of—both the dark and the light—and where ideologies of separation and division eventually lead us.

Peter had found two fantastic cameramen from Warsaw who would secure all the necessary permits and permissions and travel down to Kraków and Auschwitz to capture the journey. We picked Peter up at Warsaw Chopin Airport and headed to our hotel, where we would meet the film crew. We learned that the Auschwitz concentration camp was located inside what the Germans called an "interest zone." This was an area of roughly fifteen square miles from which the inhabitants were expelled in an attempt by the camp authorities to remove witnesses to the crimes and impede contact between prisoners and the outside world. The hotel we stayed in was about half a mile from the camp and well inside this zone.

The following morning, we made our way to the Auschwitz-Birkenau Memorial and Museum and met up with our guide, Maria, who would spend the next two days with us as we explored and discussed what had happened at Auschwitz I, the main concentration camp, and the much larger expansion of Auschwitz II-Birkenau, the nearby combined concentration/extermination camp. Maria was Jewish and had family members who perished in the camps. Her mental anguish surrounding her loss had stemmed from questions—that remained unanswered—about why it happened, how it could happen, and what makes people commit such atrocities. To help her cope, Maria decided her calling was to educate people about the horrors that occurred in this place.

At the beginning of our day we chatted and got to know each other. As Maria and I started to have a discussion on camera, standing less than three feet apart, looking each other directly in the eye, I had a hard time staying present. The answers to her questions about why I was there, my history, how I got into and out of the white supremacist movement were automatic. I was answering them in the same way I had answered them a hundred times before. This was keeping the conversation in my head, and it really needed to go deeper and be from the heart. Peter noticed this and skilfully challenged me by calling me out on my autonomic responses, and we were able to start the conversation over but in a different way. I recognized there was still a part of me that didn't want to confront and connect with what I was going to experience that day.

We then began the tour around Auschwitz. We passed through the gates that read *Arbeit macht frei*, which translates to "Work will set you free," a cynical lie, as the prisoners confined there would mostly only be freed by death. I was reminded of the cold, disconnected gallows humour we had in the white supremacist movement when we would joke that next time, it would say, "Nothing will set you free." So many years ago, thousands of miles away, dispassionately looking at books or TV and immersed in neo-Nazi ideology, my mind had been capable of thinking these things, but standing in the middle of this death camp, on the ground where millions had been systematically murdered, feeling the infinite sorrow of the place, it was hard to imagine the despicable state of mind that could come up with such unthinkable attempts at humour.

As we passed through the gates toward the prisoners' barracks, Maria paused to point out where the camp orchestra used to play. The orchestra (and the swimming pool, which was actually used as a water reservoir) are habitually used by Holocaust deniers as proof that Auschwitz was more like a holiday camp, all fun and games, and not a death camp. The reality is the orchestra was used to get the prisoners to march in time so that they could be counted more easily.

After exploring several of the administrative buildings, it was time to enter Block 5, the former barracks that now holds the artifacts. Each room had, behind its protective glass, relics that had remained at the camp since it was liberated by the Soviet army in 1945. In one room, there was a huge tangled mass of eyeglasses. Another room was filled with shoes. I took the time to take in the gravity of what was before me. I was struck at noticing little children's shoes, and I thought of my own children and how they had saved me. There was a room filled with cups, plates, cutlery, and teapots, the belongings of people who believed they were going to be resettled in the East, as the Germans claimed in order to disguise the true intention of the deportations. The next was a room filled with suitcases, each with an address and often the birthdate of the owner.

Here was a physical reminder of the story my financial services client Alan had told me about how his mother always had a suitcase by the front door, ready to leave at a moment's notice. I've heard variations of this story many times now. For Jewish people, suitcases have a meaning and significance that I had never considered, and my actions meant that those suitcases could never be put away.

I stood silently and took in the display of suitcases before me. I wanted to feel these rooms, not just see them. Throughout the

experience, I felt apprehension, nervousness, the desire to be somewhere else, and a healthy sense of shame about the things I had said
and done to harm Jews. Being in this place was a tragic reminder of
where extremist ideology goes if left unchecked. The shame came
in different waves and intensities throughout the day, and facing
this room of suitcases, I felt it strongly, the shame burning just a
half inch beneath the skin of my chest. But this room also filled me
with another feeling, and that was a sense of abject hopelessness. It
was palpable. I couldn't imagine the total hopelessness the owners
of these suitcases would have felt when they discovered that instead
of being resettled, they had in fact been brought to their deaths.

The last room was the most difficult for me. Standing in front
of the glass, I could see a long room filled with human hair. The
hair of 30,000 women: ponytails, braids, long hair, short hair, all
different colours and textures. Understandably, out of respect,
photos of this room are no longer allowed. Nausea, revulsion, and
disgust overwhelmed me, and the deep shame was searing. For
the next twenty minutes, my mind was out of the picture, and I
simply allowed myself to feel absolutely everything, no matter how
uncomfortable, and process it.

Feeling heavy and somewhat drained, I left the room to go back
outside where Maria was waiting. After ten minutes, as I described
my experience to her, Peter stepped in with a question. As part of
the preparation for this trip, I had asked several people around
me, especially Dõv, who has the uncanny ability to deliver zingers
that are as revealing as they are uncomfortable, to come up with
questions to ask me at various points during the tour. I wouldn't
know these questions in advance—the idea being that this process
would help me go deeper on my path of inward investigation and
healing and experience a new level of discomfort. Peter, who has

an extensive counselling background, sensed the perfect moments to deliver them.

"Imagine a young boy here, a prisoner, about age nine or ten, and also imagine yourself here, age nine or ten. If you were the prisoner, what would you say to yourself?"

"Don't be an asshole," I replied as I contemplated the scenario.

Age ten was when I had walked in on my father betraying my mother, which was the trauma that began my descent into emotional disconnection and numbness. All of the guilt, shame, anger (at myself), and sorrow were swirling through me, and I was lost for words.

Peter then flipped the question around: "What would you say to the little boy who's a prisoner here?"

I thought deeply about how to reply, all the while holding direct eye contact with Maria. But no words came.

"I don't know," I finally said. "How do you offer words of hope to someone whose situation is so utterly hopeless?"

"That's easy," Maria replied. "'I will remember you. I will not forget. And I will ensure you will not be forgotten.'"

As soon as Maria spoke her last word, I felt a flood of emotions overtake me, and my eyes filled with tears. In my mind, as I repeated those words, saying them to the boy, I was also saying them to Little Tony. For a long time, I did not remember him and he was forgotten. Envisioning the little boy saying those words made me connect to my core like a lightning rod resonating deep within me. As I remembered my own pain and abandonment, and the way I had abandoned Little Tony, I was also committing to remembering for that boy of my imagination and the others who had died here. In that moment, my perception and understanding became very real, and I solidified my emotional connection to that place.

During this epiphany, Maria and I looked into each other's eyes. The look on her face, and how she held herself, made it clear that this was also very difficult and challenging for her. Maria had told me she'd done a lot of work on herself, and it showed. I am forever grateful for the gifts she gave me. She was able to challenge me and hold the space for me, be with me on that journey without judgment, for as long as I needed.

At the end of the day, we found ourselves at the gas chamber and crematorium at Auschwitz I, which operated from August 1940 to July 1943, until the establishment at Auschwitz II-Birkenau of additional crematoria and gas chambers to handle the sheer volume of victims. Seeing the restored crematorium in person put my previous Holocaust denials to shame.

The next day, when Maria greeted us at Auschwitz, I noticed that her demeanour had changed. No longer was she apprehensive and a bit guarded. She was now more enthusiastic and open. She had spent many hours the night before discussing the events of the day with her husband, and it seemed like that debrief, combined with our deep conversations the previous day as she observed me struggling to process my experience, convinced her of the sincerity of my intentions.

We met Maria at six a.m. and were given access to both camps for two hours prior to the museum opening to the public so that we could film without tourists present. Finally, we made the journey to Birkenau, five minutes away. Birkenau, with its iconic entrance where the rail lines go straight through an archway in the gatehouse and into the middle of the camp. Construction of Auschwitz II-Birkenau began in October 1941 to ease congestion at the main camp. As we walked beside one of the barbed-wire fences with its guard towers, we arrived at a corner of the camp and surveyed all the buildings that were still standing and the chimneys of those that weren't. Birkenau was massive, the sheer scale mindblowing. It was in this corner of the camp that I began to comprehend the vast magnitude, the size and complexity, of this operation that had been dedicated to one goal: the genocide of the Jewish people.

This place wasn't a camp; it was a highly complex and intricate machine with many moving parts. To make this place function required an enormous logistical operation and bureaucracy, and it was just one piece of an even larger puzzle. We had started this trip in Budapest, where we had seen the buildings of the Jewish quarter without the people who had once lived there, an entire community that had been made to disappear in a scenario that played out elsewhere in cities across Europe, in a carefully orchestrated plan of total extermination that ended here, right where I was standing.

As I stood there, the remnants as far as the eye could see through the barbed-wire fence, I finally began to understand what this place truly was. And with that understanding, that feeling of nausea returned, accompanied by disgust and revulsion, and, of course, my old friend shame. The mixture of these feelings was new to me, and I had to pause to take it all in. In that moment, for the first time, I connected that nausea, disgust, and revulsion directly to the things I had said and done as a Holocaust denier and disseminator of anti-Semitic propaganda in the white supremacist movement. Before, I had been intellectually disgusted not so much for who I was—because I had developed self-compassion for that—but for the things I had said and done. Now, I felt that disgust and revulsion deeply connect to my previous activities, and I had to own those feelings at a deep emotional level. It took physically witnessing the external evidence of the horror of this place for me to connect emotionally to the horrific things I'd said and done.

In this state of total openness in a safe space that Maria held for me, I looked at the attempts by me and other Holocaust deniers to negate and cover up this historical crime. In so doing, was I in some way an accessory after the fact in cleaning up and hiding the crime so many decades later? Looking right at Maria, I acknowledged that in another time and another place, given the ideology that I'd held, I could have been a guard in this camp. It is essential to recognize that just as the potential to be a guard had lain within me, the potential to be a guard rests within everyone given the wrong set of pressures and circumstances; in fact, it is that recognition that leads to vigilance and a path to ensure it doesn't happen again. We must first accept the very dark nature that exists within humanity, because if we allow ourselves to deny or forget, we are doomed to repeat. As Mark Twain is thought to have said, "History doesn't repeat itself but it often rhymes." As dark clouds gather again over Europe (and the whole of the Western world), as far-right and fascist parties rise up, we must never forget where the politics of fear and hate can and will lead us.

As we continued the tour of the expanded camp, which was never completed, it became evident that as big as this operation was, it wasn't meant to permanently house the sheer number of people who were sent here. It was a killing hub essential to the Final Solution, the German plan to kill the Jews of Europe. More than 1.1 million people were murdered at Auschwitz, including Poles, Roma, Soviet prisoners of war, and nearly 1 million Jews. As we walked back to the centre of the camp along the infamous railway tracks, we came upon Kremas II and III. Destroyed by the Nazis at the end of the war, the two gas chamber and crematorium complexes remain monuments as rubble.

As I sat there, feeling the familiar healthy shame and guilt combined with disgust and nausea that kept creeping back, Peter asked me another one of Dōv's incisive questions:

"Imagine the families of all those who died here. What would you to say to them?"

I was hit with a flood of emotions. But by far the most powerful was a deep, deep sense of shame. My eyes welled with tears.

"Sorry," I said to Marie as our gazes locked again. "I'm so incredibly sorry and deeply ashamed about the things I said and did, and ashamed for sharing untruths about their truth. That they didn't deserve anything that had happened to them, and that people like me made light of it or denied it makes a second crime against those people. I don't think I am in a position to ask for forgiveness, as it's not about me. I will bear witness for them, and I will remember who they are and what happened here so that no one forgets. That is my *tshuvah*."

Maria asked me what would have happened if I'd come to Auschwitz twenty or thirty years ago. Would it have changed my mind about Holocaust denial and white supremacist ideology? To that I had to honestly answer no. During that time in my life, I was too emotionally numb to have been able to feel this place, too arrogant, with too much invested in my identity that was wrapped around white supremacist ideology, to be able to admit that I could be wrong.

Maria was so present and there with me, providing the space for me to process so much while doing so much processing of her own. We were both transformed by the encounter. She later shared her own initial trepidation and discomfort at what our two days together would entail, and how much she learned and processed. As much as she gave me permission to ask her anything, that permission was reciprocated on my part, and I shared everything about my path, leaving her perhaps better prepared to handle similar questions in the future. Our relationship, though short, will be one of the deepest and most powerful in my lifetime.

She also asked me if I could be a guard now, to which I also answered no. I do not think that is possible now, with the expanded consciousness and awareness I have. I would rather lose my life than lose my soul.

CHAPTER 12

LIFE AFTER HATE

AFTER LAUNCHING LIFE AFTER Hate in 2011, we did the best we could for a few years with our good intentions and the lint in our pockets. In 2014, I travelled to Europe on a two-pronged mission; first, to learn from the experienced and established exit organizations that help people disengage from extremist groups and deradicalize; and second, to build support for Angela King's ideas for the development of an assessment tool to evaluate where former extremists were in their leaving process. We also started to share our insights and knowledge with academic institutions and governments to help them understand the problem of violent extremism from our unique perspective. We shared our stories so that others could learn from them and avoid following in our footsteps to perpetrate violence and damage communities.

Soon after I returned from Europe, we received a research grant to fund Angela's assessment tool from the National Institute of Justice (NIJ), the research arm of the US Department of Justice, led by the Research Triangle Institute. We facilitated research interviews with forty-eight former white supremacists with some of the top academics in the field of violent extremism: professors of sociology Dr Pete Simi and Dr Kathleen Blee. Each interview was a full six-to-eight-hour life inventory geared to trying to understand some of the different pathways in and out of violent far-right extremism. Again, many familiar themes emerged for both going into and coming out. The study had an unusually large sample of women to interview (one-third of the subjects were women, far higher than in previous research efforts), and it was interesting to note the significance that a romantic relationship can play for women in both joining and leaving white supremacist groups, which was something I had witnessed while I was still in the movement, and which I had also heard anecdotally from women after they left.

In the aftermath of the 2012 massacre at the Sikh temple in Oak Creek, Wisconsin, Life After Hate rose to prominence in the media through interviews and providing outreach to the affected communities to offer support and bear witness to the tragedy. The mass shooting in 2015 of nine African Americans at the Emanuel African Methodist Episcopal Church in Charleston, South Carolina, saw the group doing similar work. Life After Hate is often asked for comment on such devastating events, being the only organization founded by former extremists to defuse the ticking time bomb of domestic violent far-right extremism. With so much government and law enforcement attention focused on potential terrorist acts from international sources such as ISIS and al Qaeda—which includes heavy surveillance of mosques and monitoring of rampant Islamophobia—authorities have taken their eye off the growing threat of domestic terrorism represented by the violent far right. Research by the Anti-Defamation League has found that from 2007 to 2016, a range of domestic extremists of all kinds were responsible for the deaths of at least 372 people across the United States. Seventy-four percent of these murders were committed by right-wing extremists such as white supremacists, sovereign citizens, and militia adherents. In 2019, the case can be made that domestic terrorism is by far a greater threat to national security than international terrorism.

In 2015, I moved from the board of directors of Life After Hate to the executive director position on a volunteer basis. In this role,

I oversaw successful counter-narrative campaigns, expansion of our outreach programs, and continued research. For outreach we conduct online and offline interventions, and coach and mentor people to leave and who have left white supremacy behind. We also often refer people to professional counselling and mental health services. We were one of three organizations selected by the Institute for Strategic Dialogue (ISD) to receive resources to create four videos designed to inspire disillusionment and create engagement within the white supremacist movement. The ISD tracked all of the activty and issued a comprehensive report on the success of our efforts. One of the one-minute videos the team produced went on to win a regional Emmy Award for public service announcement. In 2016, we applied for four grants from the Department of Homeland Security's Countering Violent Extremism Program, which focuses on funding community groups engaged in prevention and outreach. In 2017, in the final days of the Obama administration, we were awarded a grant for $480,000 for US-based interventions (though we do help people outside of the United States in places like Canada).

In anticipation of receiving our award and beginning a project of online interventions where we would engage white supremacists on social media platforms—and have those interventions evaluated academically—we started professionalizing the organization. Our slogan for 2017 was "Going Pro," as we looked to step up every aspect of our operation, from accounting systems to policies and processes. Smaller donations from individuals started to trickle in, and in April 2017, we received our largest donation ever; it came from Colin Kaepernick, the African American National Football League star who inspired controversy by taking a knee during the American national anthem to signify his support for the Black Lives Matter movement and in protest of the systemic oppression of African American people and people of colour, especially at the hands of law enforcement.

With the smaller donations, the big Kaepernick donation, and the pending Department of Homeland Security (DHS) grant (which was now unfortunately under review and re-evaluation by the Trump administration), we were finally able, for the first time, to make the executive director role a paid position. My first act of business was to fire myself and hire Sammy Rangel because of his extensive counselling experience (a master's in social work and eighteen years' experience), his ability to train others in basic one-to-one counselling, and his expertise running programs. Sammy designed and ran a very successful prison re-entry program in Wisconsin that reduced the recidivism rate of thirty-six percent to six percent with some of the most difficult inmate populations. The three-year rate went from more than seventy percent down to six percent, as measured by the Alfred Adler Institute.

One of Sammy's first actions was to adopt the social work code of ethics as the guiding document for how Life After Hate would run its outreach program. This document included guidelines on client privacy, confidentiality, and a whole host of best practices that put the clients' interests first. I moved back to the board of directors, which consisted of three co-founders, who all stepped down as we recruited well-respected experts in the study of violent extremism, thus giving up control of the organization to establish transparency and accountability. (Life After Hate now has a Platinum rating on GuideStar, the consumer guide for charities and non-profits.)

On August 11–12, 2017, thousands of alt-right protestors from dozens of organizations that included neo-Nazis, the KKK, neo-Confederates, militias, and other assorted white supremacists gathered for a "Unite the Right" rally in Charlottesville, Virginia.

The weekend began with hundreds of young men, many of them clean-cut, wearing polo shirts and khaki pants, marching through the University of Virginia campus in a torch-lit procession reminiscent of Nazi rallies in Nuremberg in 1935, or, more recently, neo-Nazi marches in Ukraine. They chanted, "You will not replace us!" And as the procession continued on its way to a controversial Confederate statue, that chant became "Jews will not replace us!" The country (and indeed the world) was horrified at the spectacle that was unfolding on national television.

The next day, all hell broke loose. The more extreme organizations came prepared for battle, wearing helmets and carrying shields emblazoned with runes and symbols from a bygone era in a show of force that displayed openly the hate and racism that was bubbling beneath the surface and at the fringes of society. Force was met with force as the day degenerated into pitched battles between protestors and counter-protestors, and riot police with pepper spray. The conflict culminated when James Alex Fields Jr. deliberately drove a Dodge Challenger into a crowd of anti-racist protestors, killing activist Heather Heyer.

The Charlottesville rally and its ramifications were a wake-up call—not the kind you can hit the Snooze button on but the kind that drags you out of the cozy comfort of your bed kicking and screaming. The Unite the Right rally shocked the world with a very public display of some of the most virulent neo-Nazi, white supremacist, far-right, and alt-right groups in a stark reminder that violent extremist ideology, if left unchecked, always results in murder.

Six weeks before the shocking events in Charlottesville, the Trump administration rescinded our DHS grant. It was clear these two things were connected. On the one hand, rescinding the grant was a message from the US government that white supremacists were not a problem that required funding. On the other, there was the reality of the unprecedented violence that surrounded the Unite the Right rally. Media attention on Life After Hate went viral, and over the next six months we received twice as much money in donations as had been promised by the grant. Almost 10,000 people donated small amounts so that we could continue our efforts to disarm violent white supremacist groups by helping their members leave.

When the co-founders started Life After Hate in 2011, it was with the simple intention of helping people who were where we once were. At that time, we could offer little more than coaching and mentoring. The role of former extremists who aren't professionally trained counsellors (like we, and most others, were) in the disengagement and deradicalization process is crucial and effective, as the shared lived experience provides a commonality that can quickly build trust.

Because of the internal work that I've done in group settings observing hundreds of people break down and break through the shackles of their past and the ego conditioning that followed—just like I had—it's sometimes easy for me to recognize and identify the patterns that are so often repeated. I have made the naive mistake of thinking that I could open someone up and help them recognize their wounds so that I could then help them heal and move forward. The first part is relatively easy; the hard part is what follows, particularly if they aren't ready. I think it is better to be blissfully unaware of our wounds and conditioning than to be taken down into our subconscious and encounter something in ourselves that we are not yet prepared to deal with, to acknowledge, to process, and to heal.

I learned this lesson through the work I did with Dōv, before my involvement in Life After Hate. This was why, in the fall of 2017, we hired Robert Orell to bring his wealth of experience and training from fourteen years working with Exit Sweden to run Life

After Hate's ExitUSA program to help members safely leave racist, violent, and extremist groups. It is vitally important to involve trained professionals like Sammy Rangel and Robert Orell in our work at Life After Hate.

The leadership at Life After Hate are much more than "formers"; they are trained professionals whose practice and knowledge are informed by their unique vantage point. What is a former? Someone who has left a white supremacist or hate group, whether yesterday, six months ago, two years ago, or twenty years ago. Is a former who's gone through extensive healing work the same as someone who has been out for the same length of time but hasn't properly healed? Formers can be very good and very credible messengers in efforts to eradicate violent extremism and its advocates, but when is the right time to use them as such? Untrained formers excel as the initial point of contact, but they are best used in the early stages of disengagement and deradicalization; professionals can take over from there to help with the deeper emotional work of self-reflection, self-awareness, vulnerability, and healing. It is important to know where the role of the former begins, but it's more important to know where it ends.

There have been some high-profile instances where formers were thrust into the public eye too soon in their journey to leave extremism behind, only to have those efforts blow up spectacularly because the former wasn't ready. Again, when someone joins a violent extremist group they, in effect, excommunicate themselves from friends, family, and society. When they leave, they have to do the same, but old friends, family, and society aren't waiting for them with open arms. That trust has been broken and needs to be rebuilt, and as such, they have to spend time in the "void," where often they not only have no friends but also no identity, for that too must be left behind in order for the journey out to be successful. This is where formers can really play a role, offering the support of community to those who are in that early stage of the process. Over time, those who have chosen to leave extremism behind eventually develop a new sense of who they are, a new identity with which to engage the world and the people in it in a healthy way. If the person is exposed to cameras and media attention early on, before a healthy new identity has been established, "former" becomes their identity, and they can become trapped in it for life, unable to continue the healing process. Life After Hate has been approached dozens of times about shooting an "intervention"-type reality TV series, but after sober reflection, we don't believe it is ethical. Based on what we know about the potential harm done to formers if they are subjected to attention too early in the process, the decision to turn down such projects is easy.

Today, Life After Hate supports individuals who wish to leave white supremacist groups, the families of people who are/were involved in those groups, and communities facing the threat of active organized white supremacists and groups in their midst. We also provide training and education to law enforcement, mental health workers, and policymakers that consists of cultural competency training in order to better understand those they will be dealing with, as well as the counselling method of motivational interviewing geared especially to helping members of hate groups wishing to leave. In the fifteen months following the Charlottesville rally, Life After Hate's ExitUSA program supported 135 requests for assistance from individuals and families from thirty different states. In addition, we corresponded with twenty-five prison inmates, and supported seventy-five individuals through our online support network and forums.

You might ask: How can the work done by Life After Hate be expanded from servicing 241 people to thousands and beyond? A lot of the methods I have described here are very resource intensive, with a lot of one-to-one interactions. For us to make a dent in the problem of increasing violent extremism and white supremacy, we have to scale up. We have started addressing this through our evidence-based training and practice that we share with those working in mental health, social work, probation, and law enforcement. Sometimes we struggle to find resources such as mental health services for people in their city or town because those available are too afraid to work with someone who has a swastika tattoo. There is a need for cultural competency training to overcome such stigmas so that more service providers can engage in this work. We now train and assist professionals, practitioners, and law enforcement who might encounter these individual to recognize them and to engage them in the most effective manner. These early contacts can determine the success or failure of these encounters and interventions.

Life After Hate cannot solve all of the world's problems around racism; however, we are an important piece operating in a very specific niche, and we have learned many lessons that can help and inform others. After Charlottesville, a creative agency from Seattle named Possible approached us to partner with them to reduce hate speech on the internet. They were inspired by Exit Germany, which for several years raised money for the fight against racism with a walkathon of sorts. The German town of Wunsiedel, where Nazi leader Rudolf Hess was buried, attracts a march of hundreds of neo-Nazis each year. In an initiative dubbed "Nazis against Nazis," locals residents and businesses were asked to sponsor the march by donating ten euros to Exit Germany for every three feet the Nazis marched. The townspeople lined the route, handing out water bottles and bananas to encourage the marchers to go a greater distance. Banners read, *If Only the Führer Knew*, as more than 10,000 euros was raised.

Life After Hate collaborated with Possible to do something similar online that targeted certain phrases and language. In 2017, there were more hate speech posts on Twitter than posts about Major League Baseball, the Super Bowl, and *Game of Thrones* combined. We identified six different degrees of hate speech and focused only on the most egregious examples—not dog whistles but tweets that had no deniability. Dog whistles are when political messages use coded language that offers one innocuous meaning to the general public and quite another meaning to the messenger's constituents. Using artificial intelligence (AI) and machine learning, Possible went to work, and the results were intriguing. The AI scanned every tweet on Twitter and flagged the posts that met the criteria for hate speech. Then, as part of the machine learning process, a human double-checked the AI's findings and determined whether the message met the criteria. If the post was confirmed, the AI sent a reply that said, "This message has been deemed to be hate speech and has been countered, if you retweet this, we will make a donation to a nonprofit dedicated to combating racism." In the first three months, the results were incredible: a 68 percent reduction in retweets and an 18 percent self-deletion rate by the author, with 7.2 million tweets prevented. Longer term, the results were a 48.7 percent reduction in collective retweets and a 45.6 percent reduction in the collective reach of hateful tweets identified. Importantly, this result was achieved without censorship. In the end, it came down to the poster's choice: to let it stand (and thus give a donation to Life After Hate), to not retweet, or to delete their own message.

Life After Hate collaborates not only with tech companies and community partners to help shape their responses to the challenges of racism and white supremacy but also with academic institutions that want to study the phenomenon, like the NIJ-funded research interviews that helped us to better understand the pathways into and out of violent extremism. And we are currently engaged in research exploring how people are getting radicalized online. We endeavour to operate with as much evidence-based practice as possible, and where there is no evidence available, we engage academics to measure, evaluate, and create new evidence-based methods where possible.

In 2017, Life After Hate was selected by Facebook/Oculus, a leading company in virtual reality, as one of ten non-profits to participate in the second year of VR for Good, an initiative that pairs ten non-profits with promising up-and-coming virtual reality filmmakers to make VR experiences that showcase the need for social change. Our filmmaker, Gabriela Arp, masterfully re-created Life After Hate co-founder Angela King's story in an eight-minute documentary called *Meeting a Monster* that puts the viewer in King's strictly conservative Christian home as a child, in the classroom getting bullied, and in prison, where she was challenged and ultimately befriended by a group of Jamaican women inmates. The VR experience generates viewer empathy for someone one might deem to be irredeemable. The documentary was selected as one of thirty-eight VR films for the 2018 Tribeca Film Festival and then as one of four films that Tribeca curated for the Cannes Film Festival. The partnership with Facebook/Oculus has given Life After Hate a valuable tool to use in our training to help mental health practitioners overcome their fears and humanize a community in need of service. There is no limit to the effective projects to address the challenge of racism and violent extremism in our society when creative minds from film, tech, and activist communities are informed by our collective lived experience, knowledge, and research.

At Life After Hate, we received a letter from a distraught mother who had an eighteen-year-old son with Asperger's syndrome. His mother said that her son was obsessed with white supremacy groups online. But what frightened her the most was that this community of white supremacists had accepted and embraced her son in a way that nobody else had done in his entire life. Approval and belonging are very deep emotional and psychological drivers that go far beyond the pull of ideology.

We receive numerous inquiries from families seeking help dealing with a loved one: many are from parents seeking help for a child who is flirting with or adopting extreme racist ideologies, who is looking for community in online white supremacy groups. If you wait for your child to walk through the front door with a high-and-tight haircut and a swastika tattoo, it is almost certainly too late; by this stage the problem is beyond the skill set of most parents. If you are a parent in this situation, the best thing you can do is engage your child early, with curiosity, non-judgment, and open communication. Find out who they are, how they see themselves in the world, and what they believe. Create a safe space for them to be open with you long before they encounter dark, hateful ideologies. It is from this space that you can sense if things are starting to go wrong.

Drawing lines in the sand often escalates a situation, as the young brain is hard-wired to cross them. The approach should be less about controlling the person and more about establishing healthy values, boundaries, and consequences. We may love our children unconditionally, yet our relationship with them can be very conditional.

For parents dealing with a child who is fully engaged in the white supremacist scene, the difficulty is that identity and ideology have become intertwined. If you challenge the ideology, by disputing or arguing facts, for example, then you are challenging the child's very identity. Most children and teens do not respond well when their identity comes under attack by any authority figure, let alone a parent: they get angry, they shut down, and they put up walls. And if we persist, they can even go so far as to sever ties and end the relationship. Once the relationship ties are severed, we have little or no influence to change things.

Given all this, we must try not to judge or reject the person or react emotionally. We reject the ideology, not the person. Sammy Rangel, the executive director of Life After Hate, taught me a great phrase: "Never concede, never condemn."

"Never concede" means to never concede our values. We need to hold firm to our values, which means we can listen to a person and neither like nor agree with what they say, just as long we do so without judgment so that we can create the foundation for understanding and healing. From there, we can mentor people through the healing activities of forgiveness, atonement, and giving back to the communities they have harmed while at the same time seeking counsellors or therapists to do much deeper healing work.

In practice, it looks like this: When we sit down with someone who wants to leave the world of racism and hate, we often simply listen to them, listen to their story, their grievance. We listen to them because, whether we agree with them or not, they perceive their beliefs as legitimate. Often, they have never had a chance to share their thoughts with someone and be heard with empathy, and that experience can be deeply cathartic. Brené Brown, who has done extensive research on shame, says: "If we can share our story with someone who responds with empathy and understanding, shame can't survive." When we genuinely listen to someone, we allow them to drop their defences and make themselves vulnerable. When a person can be vulnerable in a safe space (for me, with my children and in Dōv's office), healing and change can occur.

Helping young people who are involved in hateful ideologies means treating them with compassion, creating and holding healthy boundaries and consequences, remembering not to attack the ideology, as it is intertwined with the identity (only later, and with the help of professionals and educators, should you engage the ideology), and seeking professional advice from organizations such as Life After Hate. Seek help! Whether it be a counsellor, faith leader, social worker, or therapist, seek help. Since the root problem in most cases has little to do with ideology and a lot to do with family dynamics, often we need the help of an objective professional. Be prepared to be vulnerable and own your part too.

Most importantly, never give up on them. My mother never gave up on me, even though she despised what I believed, lost friends, had to carry the stigma in the workplace, and harboured a great deal of shame over the simple fact that she was my mother. The easiest thing she could have done would have been to condemn me and throw me under the bus. But she didn't. My mother saw the humanity in me, even when I couldn't see it myself. Nobody is irredeemable.

The more I worked on myself, the more I challenged myself with compassion and forgiveness, the more I healed, the better my relationship became with my mother and with my two children. In fact, the better most of my relationships became. Changing who we are inside also affects the people around us, for better or for worse.

The volunteer work I have done for Life After Hate has afforded me the opportunity to give back to the communities I had harmed, as well as to continue my own personal healing journey. Through making myself vulnerable by telling my story as a public speaker, I'm able to transform the horrible deeds I committed into a force for good. By helping others take a similar path, I can contribute to a collective voice for change that is becoming more powerful with every former who chooses this path. I get asked often what my children know about my history, and I answer that they know my history, but I am not my history. I am no longer trapped in all that anger and hate, spewing it on everyone around me. By sharing my story, I hope to inspire others to take the journey inward to healing and self-compassion so that they too can be a positive force in this world, whether they were in a hate group or not.

In sharing my lived experiences I can also provide understanding and expertise as we struggle to confront the horrors of multiple racially motivated mass murders that have sprung upon us like a plague in recent years. The violence and murder the white supremacist movement fantasized about all those years ago—the violence I once fantasized about—have now become a horrific reality.

CHAPTER 13
RIGHT HERE,
RIGHT NOW

ON OCTOBER 27, 2018, a gunman stormed into the Tree of Life synagogue in Pittsburgh, Pennsylvania. Shouting anti-Semitic epithets, he opened fire and killed eleven congregants and injured six people (including four police officers) in an attack that stunned the nation and the world. This was the largest mass murder of Jews on US soil ever. Shortly before the attack, the perpetrator posted on far-right social media site Gab that "HIAS [Hebrew Immigrant Aid Society] likes to bring invaders [referring to migrant caravans from Central America] in that kill our people. I can't sit by and watch my people get slaughtered. Screw your optics, I'm going in."

I had the opportunity to visit Tree of Life several months after the attack and speak to the community in Pittsburgh. As I stood at the memorial, I was reminded yet again that white supremacy and anti-Semitism (and all hateful ideologies) end in murder. I was concerned that these atrocities were happening with greater and greater frequency. Were these attacks at places of worship becoming normalized? Were we sliding that far? First the Oak Creek gurdwara, then the Charleston church, and now the Pittsburgh synagogue. Three different faiths, three different religious communities.

And then, on March 15, 2019, less than six months later, a gunman attacked two mosques in Christchurch, New Zealand, shooting and killing fifty-one and injuring fifty before being apprehended on his way to a third mosque. This massacre stunned the world.

Not only because of the sheer scale of the attack and the number of people killed (the only white supremacist mass shooting with more casualties was perpetrated by Anders Breivik, who killed sixty-nine in Norway at a youth camp in 2011), but also because the shooter livestreamed the attack; the livestream and the video of the shooting made afterwards went viral, and countless millions have viewed it. Whereas the Tree of Life shooter announced his immediate intentions on social media, this shooter strapped a small video camera to his head at the beginning of his planned slaughter. More than 8,000 people from New Zealand called the country's mental health hotline after stumbling across the video in their Facebook and Twitter feeds. As I write this in spring 2019, the video still exists online.

The Christchurch shooter, like Anders Breivik, posted a manifesto online, so we see a pattern of far-right terrorists learning and copying from each other beginning to emerge. With the attacks in North America, Europe, and New Zealand, the phenomenon is now global across regions where there is a dominant white population. Not only are these attacks inspiring like-minded individuals (not long after Christchurch, there was a shooting at a Poway, California, synagogue), but they are also inspiring their perceived enemies. In an apparent response to Christchurch, 258 Christians were killed on Easter Sunday 2019 in Sri Lanka in a bombing campaign that hit several churches and luxury hotels.

These attacks are a harbinger of things to come if we ignore or dismiss them; like I have said many times, white supremacist ideology, if left unchecked, always ends in murder. The challenge before us is immense and represents a potential existential crisis for our society. It is not going to be resolved by staying in our comfort zone. We have to change who we choose to be in every moment of every day and look into our own hearts to root out intolerance, judgment, and indeed, hate.

So how do we respond? What can the average person do? How can we most effectively respond to the presence of white supremacist and other hate groups?

My theory is that there are two main components to the growing white supremacist movement. Although it is different from the movement I once belonged to, so much of it is the same. Technology has sped up the radicalization process, and social media now acts as a message amplifier and the great connector, but the underlying psychological drivers are the same.

Firstly, and this is as true now as it was back in the day, this is not a cohesive movement. It is a loosely organized collection of small and medium organizations driven by ego and rife with infighting. Although it is easy to dismiss these groups because some of them are small and disorganized, we cannot afford to do that: all it takes is a powerful, charismatic leader to turn this ragtag collective into a mass movement. We have observed this possibility at the national level.

The first group in this movement are the traditional old-school neo-Nazis and skinheads, street thugs who love a brawl. They thrive on attention and conflict with a simple strategy of setting up shop and letting the violence come to them. They don't have to go looking for violence; they merely have to say when and where they're going to be—at a monument, a park, a government building—and the violence will follow, guaranteed. They can then claim they were attacked and play the victim card. Physically attacking them plays right into their hands, as they only know force and have very little power. I was at Boston Common the weekend after Charlottesville where 40,000 people turned out to peaceably declare, "Not in our town!" Now that was power!

Within that crowd was a tiny number dedicated to using force against the alt-right, and I saw someone who was sucker punched and had their lip torn open because somebody mistook him for a skinhead due to his shaved head. Violence begets violence; we all have the right to defend and protect ourselves, but the risks are high, including the potential for collateral damage that usually afflicts bystanders. The argument often used to justify a violent response to fascism is Hitler and the force it took to remove him from power. It also cost 70 million lives. Violence often doesn't work, as witnessed by the Spanish Civil War, which left 500,000 dead.

The violent far right thrives on two things: conflict and attention. Violence against them usually triggers an escalated response, and their capacity for violence knows no bounds. Physical force, direct action, doxxing, and the like, wielded with no rules of engagement, is a clumsy strategy; mistakes get made, and innocent people get hurt. Power versus Force. What is the power of peaceful civil disobedience and actions versus direct action and by any means necessary? Which is more effective?

According to Erica Chenoweth, a political scientist at Harvard University and author of the TEDxBoulder talk "Civil Resistance and the '3.5% Rule,'" civil disobedience is not only the moral choice; it is also the most powerful way of shaping world politics. Looking at the last hundred years, the research suggests non-violent protest achieves its goals at twice the rate of armed conflict, and those that engage a threshold of 3.5 percent of the population have never failed to bring about change. Not only is non-violent activism more successful, but it also takes much fewer resources than armed conflict. Chenoweth cites the People Power Revolution that toppled the Ferdinand Marcos dictatorship in the Philippines in four days after millions peacefully took to the streets and the Rose Revolution that ended the Soviet reign in Georgia as examples of change effected by non-violent protest. Some of the world's greatest movements for political and social change were led by famous proponents of non-violence, such as Martin Luther King Jr., Nelson Mandela, and, of course, Mohandas Gandhi.

I don't think I know anybody who left the white supremacist movement because of threats of violence. They might have altered their behaviour somewhat, to become more cautious, but they never left the movement. As Frank Meeink has told me, "Not once, when being pelted with bottles on a march, did I stop and think that my was ideology wrong." Force in this context is alluring, as it offers an instant sense of gratification, but it is costly and ineffective in the long term. Vigilante justice is not going to power the change required to heal nations.

So if the far right comes to town in search of attention and conflict, what should we do? Where possible, starve them of the reward they seek. When neighbourhoods or campuses are flyered, many communities panic and the leaflets quickly generate a media storm. Of course they do—because that is the purpose of the leaflets. A couple hundred leaflets on the windshields of cars or on the doorsteps of homes isn't likely to recruit anybody, but the media storm that follows absolutely will. Journalists and reporters need to understand the methodology behind these actions and resist falling into that trap and naming the organization behind the drive. For many of these groups, attention is like oxygen, and violence and conflict merely serve to reinforce their victim mentality.

There are many alternatives to violent confrontation: holding larger competing rallies or events, using strategies like Exit Germany's walkathon to deter participation, and building community and coalitions. It is essential that we stand for the people in our society who are the targets of the rallies and leaflets so that they know they are not alone, that they have allies, that they are indeed important and valued members of our society. We must have the courage to be active bystanders and prevent people from being further marginalized by our silence and passivity. You don't have to be aggressive and in-your-face to communicate that a phrase, a joke, or a behaviour is not okay. Although violent far-right ideology appears to live on the fringes, it is informed by mainstream acts of intolerance.

However, those who are the most visible and obvious about their racism are only the tip of the iceberg. There is a second group of people in the white supremacist movement: the online communities whose activity is mostly limited to chat rooms, 4chan, Gab, and a multitude of nooks and crannies you've never heard of on the internet. Their preferred currency is the production of countless racist memes whose goal is to trigger and enrage people. This group tends to be highly intelligent, and while many don't have the same capacity for physical violence as those in the first group, their violence is emotional and psychological, and is committed online. Although this isn't to say that this behaviour can't spill over into significant acts of violence in the real world, as we've seen with recent devastating mass shootings.

We must choose a healthy response to these attacks. For those of us combatting white supremacy, violence is a fear response, and it only adds to the fear and hate already in the world. If fear and shame are most often at the root of hate, then how can more fear and shame be the cure? Although it may seem we are hard-wired for conflict and violence, I believe the opposite to be true. If we were wired for violence, then soldiers wouldn't come home with post-traumatic stress disorder. It is necessary for those who choose violence to dehumanize themselves internally, and having been there myself, I do not wish that on anyone. That is why I advocate non-violence as a response to violent extremism. Because we are all connected.

Fear is the embodiment of disconnection, whereas love is the embodiment of connection; good is total connection, whereas evil is total disconnection. That is the lens through which I view the world, and I can acknowledge that for many years I was operating from evil and disconnection. These forces remain strong in the world today, and to counter them we must choose good, we must choose love, we must choose connection.

John Bradshaw describes toxic shame as "a spiritual disease," and I suggest that rage, fear, dehumanization, and hate are the equivalent of spiritual pollution. Just as tackling environmental pollution requires a concerted effort not just from the government but from each and every one of us, spiritual pollution is no different. Just as we all have to make a conscious effort to recycle our waste every day, everyone needs to make a conscious effort to minimize their spiritual pollution, if not reverse it. We must look into our hearts at our own unconscious biases and intolerance that provoke in us thoughts or acts of judgment, rage, and dehumanization. As Martin Luther King Jr. said in *Strength to Love*, "Returning hate for hate multiplies hate, adding deeper darkness to a night already devoid of stars. Darkness cannot drive out darkness; only light can do that. Hate cannot drive out hate; only love can do that."

A challenge? Yes. Impossible? No.

The day after the Tree of Life massacre, I stood in solidarity at the Jewish Community Centre in Vancouver to bear witness and give support. A local rabbi relayed a message from Jeffrey Myers, the rabbi of Tree of Life, whose response to the tragedy was that the world needed healing. Myers' words called to mind similar statements made by representatives of the Sikh community after the Oak Creek massacre. Here was a group stunned in their grief, yet vengeance was the last thing on their minds. Healing and peace were paramount. Both are inspiring examples of radical compassion.

Radical compassion isn't easy and it requires courage. Learning to have compassion for myself was one of the hardest things I had to do. And the hardest thing in the world is to have compassion for people who seem to have no compassion. But aren't they the ones who need it most? Will Bowen, author of *A Complaint Free World*, writes, "Hurt people hurt people. We are not being judgmental by separating ourselves from such people. But we should do so with compassion. Compassion is defined as a 'keen awareness of the suffering of another coupled with a desire to see it relieved.' People hurt others as a result of their own inner strife and pain. Avoid the reactive response of believing they are bad; they already think so and are acting that way. They aren't bad; they are damaged and they deserve compassion. Note that compassion is an internal process, an understanding of the painful and troubled road trod by another. It is not trying to change or fix that person."

Compassion is often seen as weak, and unless compassion is accompanied by healthy boundaries and consequences, it can be. Without healthy boundaries and consequences, compassion can become an invitation to abuse. Compassion is tough love and giving people what they need, and not what they want. We live in a society filled with unhealthy boundaries and consequences when we employ the tools of fear, violence, and shaming instead of operating from love, when we try to utterly destroy people online and off. When compassion is coupled with strong, healthy boundaries and consequences, we can not only keep people safe but also offer a way back to humanity. Although it is important to call people out, we must also be prepared to call people in. As Sammy Rangel says, "No one is irredeemable."

My journey of self-compassion led me to rediscover and rekindle my relationship with Little Tony, eliminating the need for the bullied ego-protector Dark Tony. I can have a few drinks now and Dark Tony is nowhere to be seen. People describe me as fun to be around, and I can make people laugh without having to cut someone down in the process. I've come to the point where God, the force, the universe, source, or whatever you want to call her represents something unknowable but something very real to me. I don't know how to describe the feeling of connectedness I get when doing a walking meditation in the woods.

The path of radical compassion has given me the courage to face my fears and my pain and embrace vulnerability, the benefits of which spill over onto other people. My life is no longer lived in the shadows of shameful secrets that used to colour my every action. Radical compassion has given me liberation to live authentically and with more freedom from my toxic shame (there is always more work to do in that area, but the rewards are so great).

Liberation and freedom aren't the point of radical compassion, however. Rather, they are the platform upon which I can live a great deal of my life in service to others. Without that platform, my capacity for true compassion and alleviating the suffering of others is negligible. I am also talking not only about alleviating the suffering of others but also the desire to change the environment that creates the suffering in the first place, the systemic causes of suffering. I can change the world more by changing who I am in the world than by trying to change the world outside of me.

SOURCES

THE FOLLOWING SOURCES WERE consulted and/or quoted in the preparation of this book.

"ADL Report Exposes Right-Wing Terrorism Threat in the U.S." ADL.com, May 22, 2017. Accessed at https://www.adl.org/news/press-releases/adl-report-exposes-right-wing-terrorism-threat-in-the-us.

Baron, Dōv. *Don't Read This ... Your Ego Won't Like It!* Burnaby, BC: Baron Mastery Institute, 2009.

Bowen, Will. *A Complaint Free World: How to Stop Complaining and Start Enjoying the Life You Always Wanted.* New York: Three Rivers Press, 2013.

Bradshaw, John. *Healing the Shame That Binds You.* Deerfield Beach, FL: Health Communications Inc., 2005.

Brown, Brené. *Daring Greatly: How the Courage to be Vulnerable Transforms the Way We Live, Love, Parent, and Lead.* New York: Penguin Random House, 2015.

———. *The Gifts of Imperfection: Let Go of Who You Think You're Supposed to Be and Embrace Who You Are.* Center City, MO: Hazelden, 2010.

Canadian Human Rights Act. R.S.C., 1985, c. H-6. https://laws-lois.justice.gc.ca/PDF/H-6.pdf.

Case, Anne, and Angus Deaton. "Mortality and Morbidity in the 21st Century." *Brookings Papers on Economic Activity* (Spring 2017): 397–476. Accessed at https://www.ncbi.nlm.nih.gov/pubmed/29033460.

Gilligan, James. *Violence: Reflections on a National Epidemic.* New York: Vintage, 1997.

Hart, William, with S.N. Goenka. *The Art of Living: Vipassana Meditation as Taught by S.N. Goenka.* New York: HarperCollins, 2009.

King Jr., Martin Luther. *Strength to Love.* Minneapolis, MN: Fortress Press, 2010.

Luskin, Fred. *Forgive for Good: A Proven Prescription for Health and Happiness.* New York: HarperCollins, 2001.

Miller, Alice. "Every Smack Is a Humiliation—A Manifesto." The Natural Child Project, 1998. Accessed at https://www.naturalchild.org/articles/alice_miller/manifesto.html.

Rohr, Richard. "Transforming Pain: Suffering—Week 1." Center for Action and Contemplation, 2018. Accessed at https://cac.org/transforming-pain-2018-10-17/.

ACKNOWLEDGMENTS

Pearse and Christina:
Without you, my heart would still be frozen.

My mother:
Who never gave up on me.

Dōv Baron:
Whose healing work made this book possible.

Rhiannon Foster:
You have stood by my side, and without your unflinching support throughout this journey, this book would not have been written. Your wisdom, guidance, and understanding have been key to completing this process that I know at times was very difficult for us both.

Thanks to Damian, all the team at Life After Hate (Robert, Angela, Sammy, Frankie, Thomas, Heather, Julie, Shelley, Dimitri, Brad), Ross and Vidhya from Moonshot, Pete Simi, Erroll Southers, Humera Khan, Brette Steele, John Picarelli, Jessika Soors and the Monkey Pack, Virginie & Onni, Katie Gorka, Indira Prahst, Gurpreet Singh, Peter Hutchison, P.J., A.A., and A.V. from TNT, Healing Tree Center in Cusco and all the schools of crazy wisdom, the leadership group of the Vancouver Velocity (Buckles, Brandy, Mal, and Alexa), and Craig "Loz" Lawrence and the RELIC community for your support and encouragement.